Welcome To The Social Media Planner

THIS PLANNER BELONGS TO:

CONTACT NUMBER:

Finding Your Ideal Customer

Do You Know Who Your Ideal Customer Is?

Do You Know Where Your Ideal Customer Hangs Out?

Your ideal customer is someone who gets their exact needs met by what you're offering

Write down 5 facebook groups where your ideal customer is likely to hangout

_____

_____

_____

_____

_____

These are the 5 places you need to be in consistently everyday giving value, interacting, etc...

Have you ever thought about this or do you just try to sell to everybody?

Do you know
Their interests/passions/hobbies
sex/age/location/their goals/their budget/their spending habits/their needs wants and desires/problems they need solving/time they are online

Hashtags

Write 4 groups of hashtags below that you can easily refer back to then enter them in your notes on your phone for copying and pasting

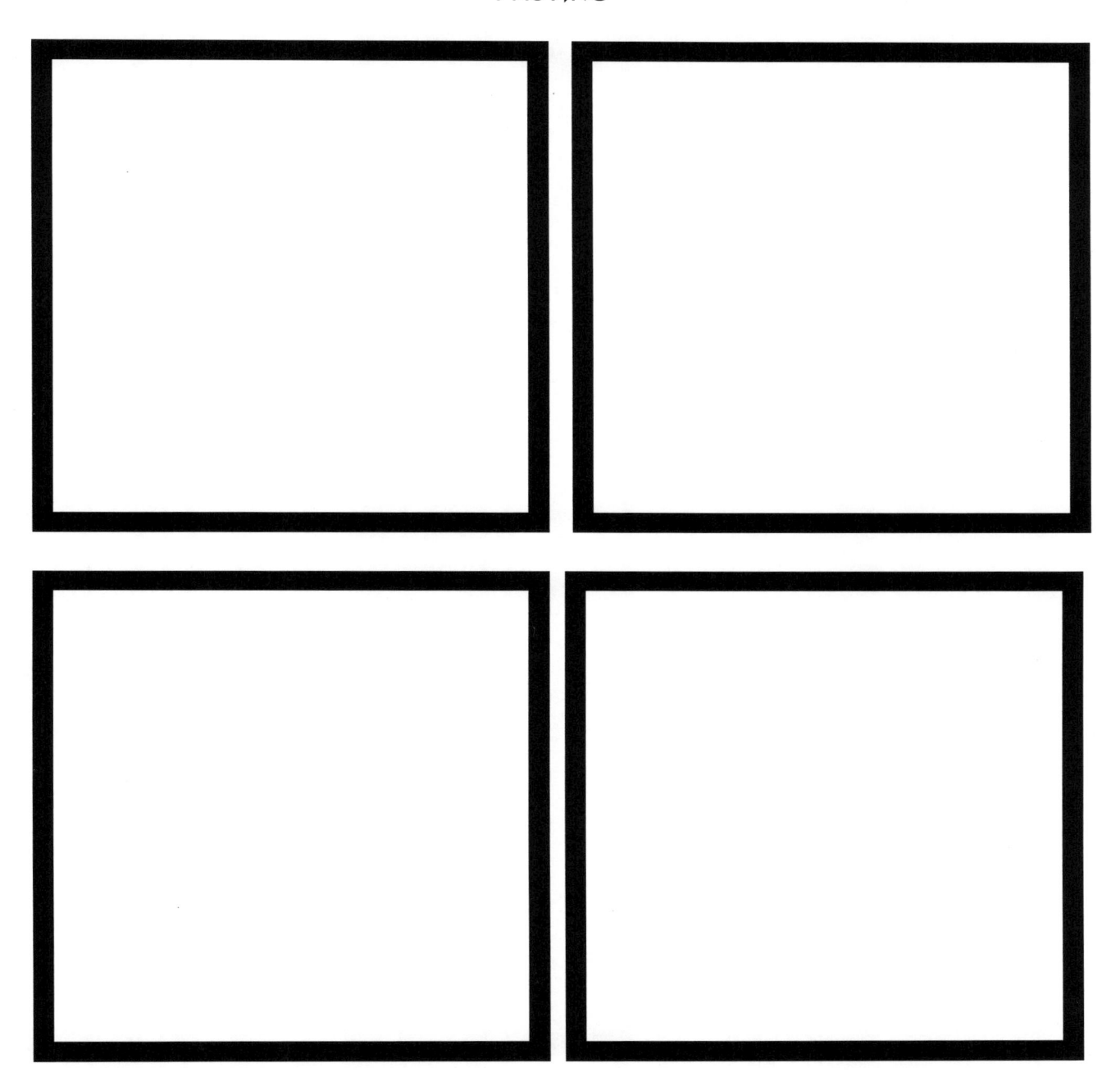

Hashtag examples you can use
#smallbusinesssaturday #supportsmallbusiness #onlinebusiness #businessowner #shoplocal
#instagood #entrepreneur #business
#homebusiness #smallbusinesslove #entrepreneursofinstagram
#dailymotivation #businesspassion #creativelifehappylife #happycustomer #shopsmall
#businessgrowth #smallbizlife #smallbiztips #smallbizlove #businesscuccess
#mindsetmatters

Your Big Ideas

An empty page for you to empty your brain so that you can jot all your big ideas for the time ahead

4 Weekly Goals

Month: _____

What Is My Main Focus: _____

What Do I Want To Earn: _____

My 5 Top Goals

When I Feel Like Giving Up I Tell Myself...

Goal: _____
Action Steps:

Deadline: _____

Goal: _____
Action Steps:

Deadline: _____

Goal: _____
Action Steps:

Deadline: _____

Goal: _____
Action Steps:

Deadline: _____

Goal: _____
Action Steps:

Deadline: _____

Weekly Content Planner

Week Commencing
_____

	Monday	Tuesday	Wednesday
Facebook	Posted ☐	Posted ☐	Posted ☐
Twitter	Posted ☐	Posted ☐	Posted ☐
Instagram	Posted ☐	Posted ☐	Posted ☐
LinkedIn	Posted ☐	Posted ☐	Posted ☐
Pinterest	Posted ☐	Posted ☐	Posted ☐
TikTok	Posted ☐	Posted ☐	Posted ☐
Snapchat	Posted ☐	Posted ☐	Posted ☐
Email	Posted ☐	Posted ☐	Posted ☐

Weekly Content Planner

Thursday	Friday	Saturday	Sunday
Posted ☐	Posted ☐	Posted ☐	Posted ☐
Posted ☐	Posted ☐	Posted ☐	Posted ☐
Posted ☐	Posted ☐	Posted ☐	Posted ☐
Posted ☐	Posted ☐	Posted ☐	Posted ☐
Posted ☐	Posted ☐	Posted ☐	Posted ☐
Posted ☐	Posted ☐	Posted ☐	Posted ☐
Posted ☐	Posted ☐	Posted ☐	Posted ☐
Posted ☐	Posted ☐	Posted ☐	Posted ☐

Month: _____

This Week's Priorities

| 1 |
| 2 |
| 3 |
| 4 |
| 5 |

Work To Do List

| 1 |
| 2 |
| 3 |
| 4 |
| 5 |

Personal To Do List

| 1 |
| 2 |
| 3 |
| 4 |
| 5 |

5 Wins

| 1 |
| 2 |
| 3 |
| 4 |
| 5 |

	Monday		Tuesday		Wednesday
Today's Affirmation / Quote		Today's Affirmation / Quote		Today's Affirmation / Quote	
Today's Goal		Today's Goal		Today's Goal	
06:00		06:00		06:00	
06:30		06:30		06:30	
07:00		07:00		07:00	
07:30		07:30		07:30	
08:00		08:00		08:00	
08:30		08:30		08:30	
09:00		09:00		09:00	
09:30		09:30		09:30	
10:00		10:00		10:00	
10:30		10:30		10:30	
11:00		11:00		11:00	
11:30		11:30		11:30	
12:00		12:00		12:00	
12:30		12:30		12:30	
13:00		13:00		13:00	
13:30		13:30		13:30	
14:00		14:00		14:00	
14:30		14:30		14:30	
15:00		15:00		15:00	
15:30		15:30		15:30	
16:00		16:00		16:00	
16:30		16:30		16:30	
17:00		17:00		17:00	
17:30		17:30		17:30	
18:00		18:00		18:00	
18:30		18:30		18:30	
19:00		19:00		19:00	
19:30		19:30		19:30	
20:00		20:00		20:00	
20:30		20:30		20:30	
21:00		21:00		21:00	

NOTES

_____

Post Ideas	Video/Vlogging Ideas	Where I'm Networking	Blogging Ideas

Pink Fizz Social

Thursday | Friday | Saturday | Sunday

	Thursday		Friday		Saturday		Sunday
Today's Affirmation / Quote		Today's Affirmation / Quote		Today's Affirmation / Quote		Today's Affirmation / Quote	
Today's Goal		Today's Goal		Today's Goal		Today's Goal	
06:00		06:00		06:00		06:00	
06:30		06:30		06:30		06:30	
07:00		07:00		07:00		07:00	
07:30		07:30		07:30		07:30	
08:00		08:00		08:00		08:00	
08:30		08:30		08:30		08:30	
09:00		09:00		09:00		09:00	
09:30		09:30		09:30		09:30	
10:00		10:00		10:00		10:00	
10:30		10:30		10:30		10:30	
11:00		11:00		11:00		11:00	
11:30		11:30		11:30		11:30	
12:00		12:00		12:00		12:00	
12:30		12:30		12:30		12:30	
13:00		13:00		13:00		13:00	
13:30		13:30		13:30		13:30	
14:00		14:00		14:00		14:00	
14:30		14:30		14:30		14:30	
15:00		15:00		15:00		15:00	
15:30		15:30		15:30		15:30	
16:00		16:00		16:00		16:00	
16:30		16:30		16:30		16:30	
17:00		17:00		17:00		17:00	
17:30		17:30		17:30		17:30	
18:00		18:00		18:00		18:00	
18:30		18:30		18:30		18:30	
19:00		19:00		19:00		19:00	
19:30		19:30		19:30		19:30	
20:00		20:00		20:00		20:00	
20:30		20:30		20:30		20:30	
21:00		21:00		21:00		21:00	

NOTES

Daily Sales | Follow Ups | Product Launches | Other Marketing

- Monday
- Tuesday
- Wednesday
- Thursday
- Friday
- Saturday
- Sunday

Pink Fizz SOCIAL

Weekly Review

Top Ideas of the Week

Useful Links and Resources

Ideas For Future Posts

Total New Followers

Checklist

- Reviewed your insights
- Live/Video/Reels - at least twice
- Reviewed your goals
- Visible in the 5 groups for your ideal customer
- Completed some personal development
- Responded to comments and messages
- Connected/networked with new people
- Responded to comments and messages
- Followed up leads
- Check in with previous customers

Weekly Insights

Did you have that lightbulb moment?

My Notes

Weekly Content Planner

Week Commencing

_____

	Monday	Tuesday	Wednesday
Facebook	Posted ☐	Posted ☐	Posted ☐
Twitter	Posted ☐	Posted ☐	Posted ☐
Instagram	Posted ☐	Posted ☐	Posted ☐
LinkedIn	Posted ☐	Posted ☐	Posted ☐
Pinterest	Posted ☐	Posted ☐	Posted ☐
TikTok	Posted ☐	Posted ☐	Posted ☐
Snapchat	Posted ☐	Posted ☐	Posted ☐
Email	Posted ☐	Posted ☐	Posted ☐

Weekly Content Planner

Thursday	Friday	Saturday	Sunday
Posted ☐	Posted ☐	Posted ☐	Posted ☐
Posted ☐	Posted ☐	Posted ☐	Posted ☐
Posted ☐	Posted ☐	Posted ☐	Posted ☐
Posted ☐	Posted ☐	Posted ☐	Posted ☐
Posted ☐	Posted ☐	Posted ☐	Posted ☐
Posted ☐	Posted ☐	Posted ☐	Posted ☐
Posted ☐	Posted ☐	Posted ☐	Posted ☐
Posted ☐	Posted ☐	Posted ☐	Posted ☐

MONTH: _____

THIS WEEK'S PRIORITIES
1	
2	
3	
4	
5	

WORK TO DO LIST
1	
2	
3	
4	
5	

PERSONAL TO DO LIST
1	
2	
3	
4	
5	

5 WINS
1	
2	
3	
4	
5	

	MONDAY	TUESDAY	WEDNESDAY
Today's Affirmation / Quote			
Today's Goal			
06:00			
06:30			
07:00			
07:30			
08:00			
08:30			
09:00			
09:30			
10:00			
10:30			
11:00			
11:30			
12:00			
12:30			
13:00			
13:30			
14:00			
14:30			
15:00			
15:30			
16:00			
16:30			
17:00			
17:30			
18:00			
18:30			
19:00			
19:30			
20:00			
20:30			
21:00			

NOTES

POST IDEAS	VIDEO/VLOGGING IDEAS	WHERE I'M NETWORKING	BLOGGING IDEAS

Pink Fizz Social

Thursday		Friday		Saturday		Sunday	
Today's Affirmation / Quote		Today's Affirmation / Quote		Today's Affirmation / Quote		Today's Affirmation / Quote	
Today's Goal		Today's Goal		Today's Goal		Today's Goal	
06:00		06:00		06:00		06:00	
06:30		06:30		06:30		06:30	
07:00		07:00		07:00		07:00	
07:30		07:30		07:30		07:30	
08:00		08:00		08:00		08:00	
08:30		08:30		08:30		08:30	
09:00		09:00		09:00		09:00	
09:30		09:30		09:30		09:30	
10:00		10:00		10:00		10:00	
10:30		10:30		10:30		10:30	
11:00		11:00		11:00		11:00	
11:30		11:30		11:30		11:30	
12:00		12:00		12:00		12:00	
12:30		12:30		12:30		12:30	
13:00		13:00		13:00		13:00	
13:30		13:30		13:30		13:30	
14:00		14:00		14:00		14:00	
14:30		14:30		14:30		14:30	
15:00		15:00		15:00		15:00	
15:30		15:30		15:30		15:30	
16:00		16:00		16:00		16:00	
16:30		16:30		16:30		16:30	
17:00		17:00		17:00		17:00	
17:30		17:30		17:30		17:30	
18:00		18:00		18:00		18:00	
18:30		18:30		18:30		18:30	
19:00		19:00		19:00		19:00	
19:30		19:30		19:30		19:30	
20:00		20:00		20:00		20:00	
20:30		20:30		20:30		20:30	
21:00		21:00		21:00		21:00	

NOTES

Daily Sales	Follow Ups	Product Launches	Other Marketing
Monday			
Tuesday			
Wednesday			
Thursday			
Friday			
Saturday			
Sunday			

Pink Fizz SOCIAL

Weekly Review

Top Ideas of the Week

Useful Links and Resources

Ideas For Future Posts

Total New Followers

Checklist

- Reviewed your insights
- Live/Video/Reels - at least twice
- Reviewed your goals
- Visible in the 5 groups for your ideal customer
- Completed some personal development
- Responded to comments and messages
- Connected/Networked with new people
- Responded to comments and messages
- Followed up leads
- Check in with previous customers

Weekly Insights

Did you have that lightbulb moment?

My Notes

Weekly Content Planner

Week Commencing
_____

	Monday	Tuesday	Wednesday
Facebook	Posted ☐	Posted ☐	Posted ☐
Twitter	Posted ☐	Posted ☐	Posted ☐
Instagram	Posted ☐	Posted ☐	Posted ☐
LinkedIn	Posted ☐	Posted ☐	Posted ☐
Pinterest	Posted ☐	Posted ☐	Posted ☐
TikTok	Posted ☐	Posted ☐	Posted ☐
Snapchat	Posted ☐	Posted ☐	Posted ☐
Email	Posted ☐	Posted ☐	Posted ☐

Weekly Content Planner

Thursday	Friday	Saturday	Sunday
Posted ☐	Posted ☐	Posted ☐	Posted ☐
Posted ☐	Posted ☐	Posted ☐	Posted ☐
Posted ☐	Posted ☐	Posted ☐	Posted ☐
Posted ☐	Posted ☐	Posted ☐	Posted ☐
Posted ☐	Posted ☐	Posted ☐	Posted ☐
Posted ☐	Posted ☐	Posted ☐	Posted ☐
Posted ☐	Posted ☐	Posted ☐	Posted ☐
Posted ☐	Posted ☐	Posted ☐	Posted ☐

MONTH: _____

This Week's Priorities

| 1 |
| 2 |
| 3 |
| 4 |
| 5 |

Work To Do List

| 1 |
| 2 |
| 3 |
| 4 |
| 5 |

Personal To Do List

| 1 |
| 2 |
| 3 |
| 4 |
| 5 |

5 Wins

| 1 |
| 2 |
| 3 |
| 4 |
| 5 |

MONDAY

Today's Affirmation / Quote

Today's Goal

| 06:00 |
| 06:30 |
| 07:00 |
| 07:30 |
| 08:00 |
| 08:30 |
| 09:00 |
| 09:30 |
| 10:00 |
| 10:30 |
| 11:00 |
| 11:30 |
| 12:00 |
| 12:30 |
| 13:00 |
| 13:30 |
| 14:00 |
| 14:30 |
| 15:00 |
| 15:30 |
| 16:00 |
| 16:30 |
| 17:00 |
| 17:30 |
| 18:00 |
| 18:30 |
| 19:00 |
| 19:30 |
| 20:00 |
| 20:30 |
| 21:00 |

TUESDAY

Today's Affirmation / Quote

Today's Goal

| 06:00 |
| 06:30 |
| 07:00 |
| 07:30 |
| 08:00 |
| 08:30 |
| 09:00 |
| 09:30 |
| 10:00 |
| 10:30 |
| 11:00 |
| 11:30 |
| 12:00 |
| 12:30 |
| 13:00 |
| 13:30 |
| 14:00 |
| 14:30 |
| 15:00 |
| 15:30 |
| 16:00 |
| 16:30 |
| 17:00 |
| 17:30 |
| 18:00 |
| 18:30 |
| 19:00 |
| 19:30 |
| 20:00 |
| 20:30 |
| 21:00 |

WEDNESDAY

Today's Affirmation / Quote

Today's Goal

| 06:00 |
| 06:30 |
| 07:00 |
| 07:30 |
| 08:00 |
| 08:30 |
| 09:00 |
| 09:30 |
| 10:00 |
| 10:30 |
| 11:00 |
| 11:30 |
| 12:00 |
| 12:30 |
| 13:00 |
| 13:30 |
| 14:00 |
| 14:30 |
| 15:00 |
| 15:30 |
| 16:00 |
| 16:30 |
| 17:00 |
| 17:30 |
| 18:00 |
| 18:30 |
| 19:00 |
| 19:30 |
| 20:00 |
| 20:30 |
| 21:00 |

NOTES

_____
_____

Post Ideas	Video/Vlogging Ideas	Where I'm Networking	Blogging Ideas

Pink Fizz SOCIAL

THURSDAY	FRIDAY	SATURDAY	SUNDAY
TODAY'S AFFIRMATION / QUOTE	TODAY'S AFFIRMATION / QUOTE	TODAY'S AFFIRMATION / QUOTE	TODAY'S AFFIRMATION / QUOTE
TODAY'S GOAL	TODAY'S GOAL	TODAY'S GOAL	TODAY'S GOAL
06:00	06:00	06:00	06:00
06:30	06:30	06:30	06:30
07:00	07:00	07:00	07:00
07:30	07:30	07:30	07:30
08:00	08:00	08:00	08:00
08:30	08:30	08:30	08:30
09:00	09:00	09:00	09:00
09:30	09:30	09:30	09:30
10:00	10:00	10:00	10:00
10:30	10:30	10:30	10:30
11:00	11:00	11:00	11:00
11:30	11:30	11:30	11:30
12:00	12:00	12:00	12:00
12:30	12:30	12:30	12:30
13:00	13:00	13:00	13:00
13:30	13:30	13:30	13:30
14:00	14:00	14:00	14:00
14:30	14:30	14:30	14:30
15:00	15:00	15:00	15:00
15:30	15:30	15:30	15:30
16:00	16:00	16:00	16:00
16:30	16:30	16:30	16:30
17:00	17:00	17:00	17:00
17:30	17:30	17:30	17:30
18:00	18:00	18:00	18:00
18:30	18:30	18:30	18:30
19:00	19:00	19:00	19:00
19:30	19:30	19:30	19:30
20:00	20:00	20:00	20:00
20:30	20:30	20:30	20:30
21:00	21:00	21:00	21:00

NOTES

DAILY SALES	FOLLOW UPS	PRODUCT LAUNCHES	OTHER MARKETING
MONDAY			
TUESDAY			
WEDNESDAY			
THURSDAY			
FRIDAY			
SATURDAY			
SUNDAY			

Pink Fizz SOCIAL

Weekly Review

Top Ideas of the Week

Useful Links and Resources

Ideas For Future Posts

Total New Followers

Checklist

- Reviewed your insights
- Live/Video/Reels - At least twice
- Reviewed your goals
- Visible in the 5 groups for your ideal customer
- Completed some personal development
- Responded to comments and messages
- Connected/Networked with new people
- Responded to comments and messages
- Followed up leads
- Check in with previous customers

Weekly Insights

Did you have that lightbulb moment?

My Notes

Weekly Content Planner

Week Commencing
_____

	Monday	Tuesday	Wednesday
Facebook	Posted ☐	Posted ☐	Posted ☐
Twitter	Posted ☐	Posted ☐	Posted ☐
Instagram	Posted ☐	Posted ☐	Posted ☐
LinkedIn	Posted ☐	Posted ☐	Posted ☐
Pinterest	Posted ☐	Posted ☐	Posted ☐
TikTok	Posted ☐	Posted ☐	Posted ☐
Snapchat	Posted ☐	Posted ☐	Posted ☐
Email	Posted ☐	Posted ☐	Posted ☐

Weekly Content Planner

Thursday	Friday	Saturday	Sunday
Posted	Posted	Posted	Posted
Posted	Posted	Posted	Posted
Posted	Posted	Posted	Posted
Posted	Posted	Posted	Posted
Posted	Posted	Posted	Posted
Posted	Posted	Posted	Posted
Posted	Posted	Posted	Posted
Posted	Posted	Posted	Posted

Month: _____

This Week's Priorities

| 1 |
| 2 |
| 3 |
| 4 |
| 5 |

Work To Do List

| 1 |
| 2 |
| 3 |
| 4 |
| 5 |

Personal To Do List

| 1 |
| 2 |
| 3 |
| 4 |
| 5 |

5 Wins

| 1 |
| 2 |
| 3 |
| 4 |
| 5 |

	Monday		Tuesday		Wednesday
Today's Affirmation / Quote		Today's Affirmation / Quote		Today's Affirmation / Quote	
Today's Goal		Today's Goal		Today's Goal	

Monday		Tuesday		Wednesday	
06:00		06:00		06:00	
06:30		06:30		06:30	
07:00		07:00		07:00	
07:30		07:30		07:30	
08:00		08:00		08:00	
08:30		08:30		08:30	
09:00		09:00		09:00	
09:30		09:30		09:30	
10:00		10:00		10:00	
10:30		10:30		10:30	
11:00		11:00		11:00	
11:30		11:30		11:30	
12:00		12:00		12:00	
12:30		12:30		12:30	
13:00		13:00		13:00	
13:30		13:30		13:30	
14:00		14:00		14:00	
14:30		14:30		14:30	
15:00		15:00		15:00	
15:30		15:30		15:30	
16:00		16:00		16:00	
16:30		16:30		16:30	
17:00		17:00		17:00	
17:30		17:30		17:30	
18:00		18:00		18:00	
18:30		18:30		18:30	
19:00		19:00		19:00	
19:30		19:30		19:30	
20:00		20:00		20:00	
20:30		20:30		20:30	
21:00		21:00		21:00	

NOTES

_____

Post Ideas	Video/Vlogging Ideas	Where I'm Networking	Blogging Ideas

Pink Fizz SOCIAL

	THURSDAY		FRIDAY		SATURDAY		SUNDAY
Today's Affirmation / Quote		Today's Affirmation / Quote		Today's Affirmation / Quote		Today's Affirmation / Quote	
Today's Goal		Today's Goal		Today's Goal		Today's Goal	
06:00		06:00		06:00		06:00	
06:30		06:30		06:30		06:30	
07:00		07:00		07:00		07:00	
07:30		07:30		07:30		07:30	
08:00		08:00		08:00		08:00	
08:30		08:30		08:30		08:30	
09:00		09:00		09:00		09:00	
09:30		09:30		09:30		09:30	
10:00		10:00		10:00		10:00	
10:30		10:30		10:30		10:30	
11:00		11:00		11:00		11:00	
11:30		11:30		11:30		11:30	
12:00		12:00		12:00		12:00	
12:30		12:30		12:30		12:30	
13:00		13:00		13:00		13:00	
13:30		13:30		13:30		13:30	
14:00		14:00		14:00		14:00	
14:30		14:30		14:30		14:30	
15:00		15:00		15:00		15:00	
15:30		15:30		15:30		15:30	
16:00		16:00		16:00		16:00	
16:30		16:30		16:30		16:30	
17:00		17:00		17:00		17:00	
17:30		17:30		17:30		17:30	
18:00		18:00		18:00		18:00	
18:30		18:30		18:30		18:30	
19:00		19:00		19:00		19:00	
19:30		19:30		19:30		19:30	
20:00		20:00		20:00		20:00	
20:30		20:30		20:30		20:30	
21:00		21:00		21:00		21:00	

NOTES

Daily Sales	Follow Ups	Product Launches	Other Marketing
Monday			
Tuesday			
Wednesday			
Thursday			
Friday			
Saturday			
Sunday			

Pink Fizz SOCIAL

Weekly Review

Top Ideas of the Week

Useful Links and Resources

Ideas For Future Posts

Total New Followers

Checklist

- Reviewed your insights
- Live/Video/Reels - at least twice
- Reviewed your goals
- Visible in the 5 groups for your ideal customer
- Completed some personal development
- Responded to comments and messages
- Connected/networked with new people
- Responded to comments and messages
- Followed up leads
- Check in with previous customers

Weekly Insights

Did you have that lightbulb moment?

My Notes

4 Weekly Reflection

Did I Achieve My Main Focus? _____   If Not Why? _____
_____

What Earnings Did You Reach? _____   Did You Reach Your Goal? _____

How Do I Feel About My Progress

3 Goals I Can Improve On

Lessons Learnt Insights Gained

3 Skills To Improve On

Which Platform Gave Most Visibility

List 5 Types of Post with the Most Engagement

4 Weekly Goals

MONTH: _____

WHAT IS MY MAIN FOCUS: _____

WHAT DO I WANT TO EARN: _____

My 5 Top Goals

When I Feel Like Giving Up I Tell Myself...

GOAL: _____

ACTION STEPS:

DEADLINE: _____

GOAL: _____

ACTION STEPS:

DEADLINE: _____

GOAL: _____

ACTION STEPS:

DEADLINE: _____

GOAL: _____

ACTION STEPS:

DEADLINE: _____

GOAL: _____

ACTION STEPS:

DEADLINE: _____

Weekly Content Planner

Week Commencing

_____

	Monday	Tuesday	Wednesday
Facebook	Posted ☐	Posted ☐	Posted ☐
Twitter	Posted ☐	Posted ☐	Posted ☐
Instagram	Posted ☐	Posted ☐	Posted ☐
LinkedIn	Posted ☐	Posted ☐	Posted ☐
Pinterest	Posted ☐	Posted ☐	Posted ☐
TikTok	Posted ☐	Posted ☐	Posted ☐
Snapchat	Posted ☐	Posted ☐	Posted ☐
Email	Posted ☐	Posted ☐	Posted ☐

Weekly Content Planner

Thursday	Friday	Saturday	Sunday
Posted	Posted	Posted	Posted
Posted	Posted	Posted	Posted
Posted	Posted	Posted	Posted
Posted	Posted	Posted	Posted
Posted	Posted	Posted	Posted
Posted	Posted	Posted	Posted
Posted	Posted	Posted	Posted
Posted	Posted	Posted	Posted

MONTH: _____

This Week's Priorities
1.
2.
3.
4.
5.

Work To Do List
1.
2.
3.
4.
5.

Personal To Do List
1.
2.
3.
4.
5.

5 Wins
1.
2.
3.
4.
5.

	MONDAY	TUESDAY	WEDNESDAY
Today's Affirmation / Quote			
Today's Goal			
06:00			
06:30			
07:00			
07:30			
08:00			
08:30			
09:00			
09:30			
10:00			
10:30			
11:00			
11:30			
12:00			
12:30			
13:00			
13:30			
14:00			
14:30			
15:00			
15:30			
16:00			
16:30			
17:00			
17:30			
18:00			
18:30			
19:00			
19:30			
20:00			
20:30			
21:00			

NOTES

Post Ideas

Video/Vlogging Ideas

Where I'm Networking

Blogging Ideas

Pink Fizz SOCIAL

	THURSDAY		FRIDAY		SATURDAY		SUNDAY
TODAY'S AFFIRMATION / QUOTE		TODAY'S AFFIRMATION / QUOTE		TODAY'S AFFIRMATION / QUOTE		TODAY'S AFFIRMATION / QUOTE	
TODAY'S GOAL		TODAY'S GOAL		TODAY'S GOAL		TODAY'S GOAL	
06:00		06:00		06:00		06:00	
06:30		06:30		06:30		06:30	
07:00		07:00		07:00		07:00	
07:30		07:30		07:30		07:30	
08:00		08:00		08:00		08:00	
08:30		08:30		08:30		08:30	
09:00		09:00		09:00		09:00	
09:30		09:30		09:30		09:30	
10:00		10:00		10:00		10:00	
10:30		10:30		10:30		10:30	
11:00		11:00		11:00		11:00	
11:30		11:30		11:30		11:30	
12:00		12:00		12:00		12:00	
12:30		12:30		12:30		12:30	
13:00		13:00		13:00		13:00	
13:30		13:30		13:30		13:30	
14:00		14:00		14:00		14:00	
14:30		14:30		14:30		14:30	
15:00		15:00		15:00		15:00	
15:30		15:30		15:30		15:30	
16:00		16:00		16:00		16:00	
16:30		16:30		16:30		16:30	
17:00		17:00		17:00		17:00	
17:30		17:30		17:30		17:30	
18:00		18:00		18:00		18:00	
18:30		18:30		18:30		18:30	
19:00		19:00		19:00		19:00	
19:30		19:30		19:30		19:30	
20:00		20:00		20:00		20:00	
20:30		20:30		20:30		20:30	
21:00		21:00		21:00		21:00	

NOTES

DAILY SALES	FOLLOW UPS	PRODUCT LAUNCHES	OTHER MARKETING
MONDAY			
TUESDAY			
WEDNESDAY			
THURSDAY			
FRIDAY			
SATURDAY			
SUNDAY			

Pink Fizz SOCIAL

Weekly Review

Top Ideas of the Week

Useful Links and Resources

Ideas For Future Posts

Total New Followers

Checklist

- Reviewed your insights
- Live/Video/Reels - at least twice
- Reviewed your goals
- Visible in the 5 groups for your ideal customer
- Completed some personal development
- Responded to comments and messages
- Connected/Networked with new people
- Responded to comments and messages
- Followed up leads
- Check in with previous customers

Weekly Insights

Did you have that lightbulb moment?

My Notes

Weekly Content Planner

Week Commencing
_____

	Monday	Tuesday	Wednesday
Facebook	Posted ☐	Posted ☐	Posted ☐
Twitter	Posted ☐	Posted ☐	Posted ☐
Instagram	Posted ☐	Posted ☐	Posted ☐
LinkedIn	Posted ☐	Posted ☐	Posted ☐
Pinterest	Posted ☐	Posted ☐	Posted ☐
TikTok	Posted ☐	Posted ☐	Posted ☐
Snapchat	Posted ☐	Posted ☐	Posted ☐
Email	Posted ☐	Posted ☐	Posted ☐

Weekly Content Planner

Thursday	Friday	Saturday	Sunday
Posted ☐	Posted ☐	Posted ☐	Posted ☐
Posted ☐	Posted ☐	Posted ☐	Posted ☐
Posted ☐	Posted ☐	Posted ☐	Posted ☐
Posted ☐	Posted ☐	Posted ☐	Posted ☐
Posted ☐	Posted ☐	Posted ☐	Posted ☐
Posted ☐	Posted ☐	Posted ☐	Posted ☐
Posted ☐	Posted ☐	Posted ☐	Posted ☐
Posted ☐	Posted ☐	Posted ☐	Posted ☐

MONTH: _____

THIS WEEK'S PRIORITIES

| 1 |
| 2 |
| 3 |
| 4 |
| 5 |

WORK TO DO LIST

| 1 |
| 2 |
| 3 |
| 4 |
| 5 |

PERSONAL TO DO LIST

| 1 |
| 2 |
| 3 |
| 4 |
| 5 |

5 WINS

| 1 |
| 2 |
| 3 |
| 4 |
| 5 |

	MONDAY	TUESDAY	WEDNESDAY
TODAY'S AFFIRMATION / QUOTE			
TODAY'S GOAL			
06:00			
06:30			
07:00			
07:30			
08:00			
08:30			
09:00			
09:30			
10:00			
10:30			
11:00			
11:30			
12:00			
12:30			
13:00			
13:30			
14:00			
14:30			
15:00			
15:30			
16:00			
16:30			
17:00			
17:30			
18:00			
18:30			
19:00			
19:30			
20:00			
20:30			
21:00			

NOTES

_____

POST IDEAS	VIDEO/VLOGGING IDEAS	WHERE I'M NETWORKING	BLOGGING IDEAS

Pink Fizz SOCIAL

THURSDAY	FRIDAY	SATURDAY	SUNDAY
TODAY'S AFFIRMATION / QUOTE	TODAY'S AFFIRMATION / QUOTE	TODAY'S AFFIRMATION / QUOTE	TODAY'S AFFIRMATION / QUOTE
TODAY'S GOAL	TODAY'S GOAL	TODAY'S GOAL	TODAY'S GOAL
06:00	06:00	06:00	06:00
06:30	06:30	06:30	06:30
07:00	07:00	07:00	07:00
07:30	07:30	07:30	07:30
08:00	08:00	08:00	08:00
08:30	08:30	08:30	08:30
09:00	09:00	09:00	09:00
09:30	09:30	09:30	09:30
10:00	10:00	10:00	10:00
10:30	10:30	10:30	10:30
11:00	11:00	11:00	11:00
11:30	11:30	11:30	11:30
12:00	12:00	12:00	12:00
12:30	12:30	12:30	12:30
13:00	13:00	13:00	13:00
13:30	13:30	13:30	13:30
14:00	14:00	14:00	14:00
14:30	14:30	14:30	14:30
15:00	15:00	15:00	15:00
15:30	15:30	15:30	15:30
16:00	16:00	16:00	16:00
16:30	16:30	16:30	16:30
17:00	17:00	17:00	17:00
17:30	17:30	17:30	17:30
18:00	18:00	18:00	18:00
18:30	18:30	18:30	18:30
19:00	19:00	19:00	19:00
19:30	19:30	19:30	19:30
20:00	20:00	20:00	20:00
20:30	20:30	20:30	20:30
21:00	21:00	21:00	21:00

NOTES

DAILY SALES

MONDAY	
TUESDAY	
WEDNESDAY	
THURSDAY	
FRIDAY	
SATURDAY	
SUNDAY	

FOLLOW UPS

PRODUCT LAUNCHES

OTHER MARKETING

Pink Fizz SOCIAL

Weekly Review

Top Ideas of the Week

Useful Links and Resources

Ideas For Future Posts

Total New Followers

Checklist

- Reviewed your insights
- Live/Video/Reels - at least twice
- Reviewed your goals
- Visible in the 5 groups for your ideal customer
- Completed some personal development
- Responded to comments and messages
- Connected/Networked with new people
- Responded to comments and messages
- Followed up leads
- Check in with previous customers

Weekly Insights

Did you have that lightbulb moment?

My Notes

Weekly Content Planner

Week Commencing
_____

	Monday	Tuesday	Wednesday
Facebook	Posted ☐	Posted ☐	Posted ☐
Twitter	Posted ☐	Posted ☐	Posted ☐
Instagram	Posted ☐	Posted ☐	Posted ☐
LinkedIn	Posted ☐	Posted ☐	Posted ☐
Pinterest	Posted ☐	Posted ☐	Posted ☐
TikTok	Posted ☐	Posted ☐	Posted ☐
Snapchat	Posted ☐	Posted ☐	Posted ☐
Email	Posted ☐	Posted ☐	Posted ☐

Weekly Content Planner

Thursday	Friday	Saturday	Sunday
Posted	Posted	Posted	Posted
Posted	Posted	Posted	Posted
Posted	Posted	Posted	Posted
Posted	Posted	Posted	Posted
Posted	Posted	Posted	Posted
Posted	Posted	Posted	Posted
Posted	Posted	Posted	Posted
Posted	Posted	Posted	Posted

MONTH: _____

This Week's Priorities
1	
2	
3	
4	
5	

Work To Do List
1	
2	
3	
4	
5	

Personal To Do List
1	
2	
3	
4	
5	

5 Wins
1	
2	
3	
4	
5	

MONDAY / TUESDAY / WEDNESDAY

Today's Affirmation / Quote

Today's Goal

Time	Monday	Tuesday	Wednesday
06:00			
06:30			
07:00			
07:30			
08:00			
08:30			
09:00			
09:30			
10:00			
10:30			
11:00			
11:30			
12:00			
12:30			
13:00			
13:30			
14:00			
14:30			
15:00			
15:30			
16:00			
16:30			
17:00			
17:30			
18:00			
18:30			
19:00			
19:30			
20:00			
20:30			
21:00			

NOTES

Post Ideas | Video/Vlogging Ideas | Where I'm Networking | Blogging Ideas

Pink Fizz SOCIAL

THURSDAY		FRIDAY		SATURDAY		SUNDAY	
TODAY'S AFFIRMATION / QUOTE		TODAY'S AFFIRMATION / QUOTE		TODAY'S AFFIRMATION / QUOTE		TODAY'S AFFIRMATION / QUOTE	
TODAY'S GOAL		TODAY'S GOAL		TODAY'S GOAL		TODAY'S GOAL	
06:00		06:00		06:00		06:00	
06:30		06:30		06:30		06:30	
07:00		07:00		07:00		07:00	
07:30		07:30		07:30		07:30	
08:00		08:00		08:00		08:00	
08:30		08:30		08:30		08:30	
09:00		09:00		09:00		09:00	
09:30		09:30		09:30		09:30	
10:00		10:00		10:00		10:00	
10:30		10:30		10:30		10:30	
11:00		11:00		11:00		11:00	
11:30		11:30		11:30		11:30	
12:00		12:00		12:00		12:00	
12:30		12:30		12:30		12:30	
13:00		13:00		13:00		13:00	
13:30		13:30		13:30		13:30	
14:00		14:00		14:00		14:00	
14:30		14:30		14:30		14:30	
15:00		15:00		15:00		15:00	
15:30		15:30		15:30		15:30	
16:00		16:00		16:00		16:00	
16:30		16:30		16:30		16:30	
17:00		17:00		17:00		17:00	
17:30		17:30		17:30		17:30	
18:00		18:00		18:00		18:00	
18:30		18:30		18:30		18:30	
19:00		19:00		19:00		19:00	
19:30		19:30		19:30		19:30	
20:00		20:00		20:00		20:00	
20:30		20:30		20:30		20:30	
21:00		21:00		21:00		21:00	

NOTES

DAILY SALES

MONDAY	
TUESDAY	
WEDNESDAY	
THURSDAY	
FRIDAY	
SATURDAY	
SUNDAY	

FOLLOW UPS

PRODUCT LAUNCHES

OTHER MARKETING

Pink Fizz SOCIAL

Weekly Review

Top Ideas of the Week

Useful Links and Resources

Ideas For Future Posts

Total New Followers

Checklist

- Reviewed your insights
- Live/video/reels - at least twice
- Reviewed your goals
- Visible in the 5 groups for your ideal customer
- Completed some personal development
- Responded to comments and messages
- Connected/networked with new people
- Responded to comments and messages
- Followed up leads
- Check in with previous customers

Weekly Insights

Did you have that lightbulb moment?

My Notes

Weekly Content Planner

Week Commencing
_____

	Monday	Tuesday	Wednesday
Facebook	Posted ☐	Posted ☐	Posted ☐
Twitter	Posted ☐	Posted ☐	Posted ☐
Instagram	Posted ☐	Posted ☐	Posted ☐
LinkedIn	Posted ☐	Posted ☐	Posted ☐
Pinterest	Posted ☐	Posted ☐	Posted ☐
TikTok	Posted ☐	Posted ☐	Posted ☐
Snapchat	Posted ☐	Posted ☐	Posted ☐
Email	Posted ☐	Posted ☐	Posted ☐

Weekly Content Planner

Thursday	Friday	Saturday	Sunday
Posted ☐	Posted ☐	Posted ☐	Posted ☐
Posted ☐	Posted ☐	Posted ☐	Posted ☐
Posted ☐	Posted ☐	Posted ☐	Posted ☐
Posted ☐	Posted ☐	Posted ☐	Posted ☐
Posted ☐	Posted ☐	Posted ☐	Posted ☐
Posted ☐	Posted ☐	Posted ☐	Posted ☐
Posted ☐	Posted ☐	Posted ☐	Posted ☐
Posted ☐	Posted ☐	Posted ☐	Posted ☐

MONTH: _____

THIS WEEK'S PRIORITIES

| 1 |
| 2 |
| 3 |
| 4 |
| 5 |

WORK TO DO LIST

| 1 |
| 2 |
| 3 |
| 4 |
| 5 |

PERSONAL TO DO LIST

| 1 |
| 2 |
| 3 |
| 4 |
| 5 |

5 WINS

| 1 |
| 2 |
| 3 |
| 4 |
| 5 |

MONDAY

Today's Affirmation / Quote:

Today's Goal:

| 06:00 |
| 06:30 |
| 07:00 |
| 07:30 |
| 08:00 |
| 08:30 |
| 09:00 |
| 09:30 |
| 10:00 |
| 10:30 |
| 11:00 |
| 11:30 |
| 12:00 |
| 12:30 |
| 13:00 |
| 13:30 |
| 14:00 |
| 14:30 |
| 15:00 |
| 15:30 |
| 16:00 |
| 16:30 |
| 17:00 |
| 17:30 |
| 18:00 |
| 18:30 |
| 19:00 |
| 19:30 |
| 20:00 |
| 20:30 |
| 21:00 |

TUESDAY

Today's Affirmation / Quote:

Today's Goal:

| 06:00 |
| 06:30 |
| 07:00 |
| 07:30 |
| 08:00 |
| 08:30 |
| 09:00 |
| 09:30 |
| 10:00 |
| 10:30 |
| 11:00 |
| 11:30 |
| 12:00 |
| 12:30 |
| 13:00 |
| 13:30 |
| 14:00 |
| 14:30 |
| 15:00 |
| 15:30 |
| 16:00 |
| 16:30 |
| 17:00 |
| 17:30 |
| 18:00 |
| 18:30 |
| 19:00 |
| 19:30 |
| 20:00 |
| 20:30 |
| 21:00 |

WEDNESDAY

Today's Affirmation / Quote:

Today's Goal:

| 06:00 |
| 06:30 |
| 07:00 |
| 07:30 |
| 08:00 |
| 08:30 |
| 09:00 |
| 09:30 |
| 10:00 |
| 10:30 |
| 11:00 |
| 11:30 |
| 12:00 |
| 12:30 |
| 13:00 |
| 13:30 |
| 14:00 |
| 14:30 |
| 15:00 |
| 15:30 |
| 16:00 |
| 16:30 |
| 17:00 |
| 17:30 |
| 18:00 |
| 18:30 |
| 19:00 |
| 19:30 |
| 20:00 |
| 20:30 |
| 21:00 |

NOTES

POST IDEAS	VIDEO/VLOGGING IDEAS	WHERE I'M NETWORKING	BLOGGING IDEAS

Pink Fizz Social

THURSDAY | FRIDAY | SATURDAY | SUNDAY

	Thursday		Friday		Saturday		Sunday
Today's Affirmation / Quote		Today's Affirmation / Quote		Today's Affirmation / Quote		Today's Affirmation / Quote	
Today's Goal		Today's Goal		Today's Goal		Today's Goal	
06:00		06:00		06:00		06:00	
06:30		06:30		06:30		06:30	
07:00		07:00		07:00		07:00	
07:30		07:30		07:30		07:30	
08:00		08:00		08:00		08:00	
08:30		08:30		08:30		08:30	
09:00		09:00		09:00		09:00	
09:30		09:30		09:30		09:30	
10:00		10:00		10:00		10:00	
10:30		10:30		10:30		10:30	
11:00		11:00		11:00		11:00	
11:30		11:30		11:30		11:30	
12:00		12:00		12:00		12:00	
12:30		12:30		12:30		12:30	
13:00		13:00		13:00		13:00	
13:30		13:30		13:30		13:30	
14:00		14:00		14:00		14:00	
14:30		14:30		14:30		14:30	
15:00		15:00		15:00		15:00	
15:30		15:30		15:30		15:30	
16:00		16:00		16:00		16:00	
16:30		16:30		16:30		16:30	
17:00		17:00		17:00		17:00	
17:30		17:30		17:30		17:30	
18:00		18:00		18:00		18:00	
18:30		18:30		18:30		18:30	
19:00		19:00		19:00		19:00	
19:30		19:30		19:30		19:30	
20:00		20:00		20:00		20:00	
20:30		20:30		20:30		20:30	
21:00		21:00		21:00		21:00	

NOTES

_____

Daily Sales | Follow Ups | Product Launches | Other Marketing

- Monday
- Tuesday
- Wednesday
- Thursday
- Friday
- Saturday
- Sunday

Pink Fizz SOCIAL

Weekly Review

Top Ideas of the Week

Useful Links and Resources

Ideas For Future Posts

Total New Followers

Checklist

- Reviewed your insights
- Live/Video/Reels - at least twice
- Reviewed your goals
- Visible in the 5 groups for your ideal customer
- Completed some personal development
- Responded to comments and messages
- Connected/networked with new people
- Responded to comments and messages
- Followed up leads
- Check in with previous customers

Weekly Insights

Did you have that lightbulb moment?

My Notes

4 Weekly Reflection

Did I Achieve My Main Focus? _____ If Not Why? _____
_____

What Earnings Did You Reach? _____ Did You Reach Your Goal? _____

How Do I Feel About My Progress

3 Goals I Can Improve On

Lessons Learnt Insights Gained

3 Skills To Improve On

Which Platform Gave Most Visibility

List 5 Types of Post with the Most Engagement

4 Weekly Goals

MONTH: _____

WHAT IS MY MAIN FOCUS: _____

WHAT DO I WANT TO EARN: _____

My 5 Top Goals

When I Feel Like Giving Up I Tell Myself...

GOAL: _____
ACTION STEPS:

DEADLINE: _____

GOAL: _____
ACTION STEPS:

DEADLINE: _____

GOAL: _____
ACTION STEPS:

DEADLINE: _____

GOAL: _____
ACTION STEPS:

DEADLINE: _____

GOAL: _____
ACTION STEPS:

DEADLINE: _____

Weekly Content Planner

Week Commencing
_____

	Monday	Tuesday	Wednesday
Facebook	Posted ☐	Posted ☐	Posted ☐
Twitter	Posted ☐	Posted ☐	Posted ☐
Instagram	Posted ☐	Posted ☐	Posted ☐
LinkedIn	Posted ☐	Posted ☐	Posted ☐
Pinterest	Posted ☐	Posted ☐	Posted ☐
TikTok	Posted ☐	Posted ☐	Posted ☐
Snapchat	Posted ☐	Posted ☐	Posted ☐
Email	Posted ☐	Posted ☐	Posted ☐

Weekly Content Planner

Thursday	Friday	Saturday	Sunday
Posted ☐	Posted ☐	Posted ☐	Posted ☐
Posted ☐	Posted ☐	Posted ☐	Posted ☐
Posted ☐	Posted ☐	Posted ☐	Posted ☐
Posted ☐	Posted ☐	Posted ☐	Posted ☐
Posted ☐	Posted ☐	Posted ☐	Posted ☐
Posted ☐	Posted ☐	Posted ☐	Posted ☐
Posted ☐	Posted ☐	Posted ☐	Posted ☐
Posted ☐	Posted ☐	Posted ☐	Posted ☐

MONTH: _____

This Week's Priorities
1.
2.
3.
4.
5.

Work To Do List
1.
2.
3.
4.
5.

Personal To Do List
1.
2.
3.
4.
5.

5 Wins
1.
2.
3.
4.
5.

	MONDAY	TUESDAY	WEDNESDAY
Today's Affirmation / Quote			
Today's Goal			
06:00			
06:30			
07:00			
07:30			
08:00			
08:30			
09:00			
09:30			
10:00			
10:30			
11:00			
11:30			
12:00			
12:30			
13:00			
13:30			
14:00			
14:30			
15:00			
15:30			
16:00			
16:30			
17:00			
17:30			
18:00			
18:30			
19:00			
19:30			
20:00			
20:30			
21:00			

NOTES

Post Ideas	Video/Vlogging Ideas	Where I'm Networking	Blogging Ideas

Pink Fizz Social

THURSDAY	FRIDAY	SATURDAY	SUNDAY
TODAY'S AFFIRMATION / QUOTE	TODAY'S AFFIRMATION / QUOTE	TODAY'S AFFIRMATION / QUOTE	TODAY'S AFFIRMATION / QUOTE
TODAY'S GOAL	TODAY'S GOAL	TODAY'S GOAL	TODAY'S GOAL
06:00	06:00	06:00	06:00
06:30	06:30	06:30	06:30
07:00	07:00	07:00	07:00
07:30	07:30	07:30	07:30
08:00	08:00	08:00	08:00
08:30	08:30	08:30	08:30
09:00	09:00	09:00	09:00
09:30	09:30	09:30	09:30
10:00	10:00	10:00	10:00
10:30	10:30	10:30	10:30
11:00	11:00	11:00	11:00
11:30	11:30	11:30	11:30
12:00	12:00	12:00	12:00
12:30	12:30	12:30	12:30
13:00	13:00	13:00	13:00
13:30	13:30	13:30	13:30
14:00	14:00	14:00	14:00
14:30	14:30	14:30	14:30
15:00	15:00	15:00	15:00
15:30	15:30	15:30	15:30
16:00	16:00	16:00	16:00
16:30	16:30	16:30	16:30
17:00	17:00	17:00	17:00
17:30	17:30	17:30	17:30
18:00	18:00	18:00	18:00
18:30	18:30	18:30	18:30
19:00	19:00	19:00	19:00
19:30	19:30	19:30	19:30
20:00	20:00	20:00	20:00
20:30	20:30	20:30	20:30
21:00	21:00	21:00	21:00

NOTES

DAILY SALES	FOLLOW UPS	PRODUCT LAUNCHES	OTHER MARKETING
MONDAY			
TUESDAY			
WEDNESDAY			
THURSDAY			
FRIDAY			
SATURDAY			
SUNDAY			

Pink Fizz Social

Weekly Review

Top Ideas of the Week

Useful Links and Resources

Ideas For Future Posts

Total New Followers

Checklist

- Reviewed your insights
- Live/Video/Reels - at least twice
- Reviewed your goals
- Visible in the 5 groups for your ideal customer
- Completed some personal development
- Responded to comments and messages
- Connected/Networked with new people
- Responded to comments and messages
- Followed up leads
- Check in with previous customers

Weekly Insights

Did you have that lightbulb moment?

My Notes

Weekly Content Planner

Week Commencing
_____

	Monday	Tuesday	Wednesday
Facebook	Posted ☐	Posted ☐	Posted ☐
Twitter	Posted ☐	Posted ☐	Posted ☐
Instagram	Posted ☐	Posted ☐	Posted ☐
LinkedIn	Posted ☐	Posted ☐	Posted ☐
Pinterest	Posted ☐	Posted ☐	Posted ☐
TikTok	Posted ☐	Posted ☐	Posted ☐
Snapchat	Posted ☐	Posted ☐	Posted ☐
Email	Posted ☐	Posted ☐	Posted ☐

Weekly Content Planner

Thursday	Friday	Saturday	Sunday
Posted ☐	Posted ☐	Posted ☐	Posted ☐
Posted ☐	Posted ☐	Posted ☐	Posted ☐
Posted ☐	Posted ☐	Posted ☐	Posted ☐
Posted ☐	Posted ☐	Posted ☐	Posted ☐
Posted ☐	Posted ☐	Posted ☐	Posted ☐
Posted ☐	Posted ☐	Posted ☐	Posted ☐
Posted ☐	Posted ☐	Posted ☐	Posted ☐
Posted ☐	Posted ☐	Posted ☐	Posted ☐

MONTH: _____

THIS WEEK'S PRIORITIES

| 1 |
| 2 |
| 3 |
| 4 |
| 5 |

WORK TO DO LIST

| 1 |
| 2 |
| 3 |
| 4 |
| 5 |

PERSONAL TO DO LIST

| 1 |
| 2 |
| 3 |
| 4 |
| 5 |

5 WINS

| 1 |
| 2 |
| 3 |
| 4 |
| 5 |

	MONDAY	TUESDAY	WEDNESDAY
Today's Affirmation / Quote			
Today's Goal			
06:00			
06:30			
07:00			
07:30			
08:00			
08:30			
09:00			
09:30			
10:00			
10:30			
11:00			
11:30			
12:00			
12:30			
13:00			
13:30			
14:00			
14:30			
15:00			
15:30			
16:00			
16:30			
17:00			
17:30			
18:00			
18:30			
19:00			
19:30			
20:00			
20:30			
21:00			

NOTES

POST IDEAS	VIDEO/VLOGGING IDEAS	WHERE I'M NETWORKING	BLOGGING IDEAS

Pink Fizz SOCIAL

THURSDAY	FRIDAY	SATURDAY	SUNDAY
TODAY'S AFFIRMATION / QUOTE	TODAY'S AFFIRMATION / QUOTE	TODAY'S AFFIRMATION / QUOTE	TODAY'S AFFIRMATION / QUOTE
TODAY'S GOAL	TODAY'S GOAL	TODAY'S GOAL	TODAY'S GOAL
06:00	06:00	06:00	06:00
06:30	06:30	06:30	06:30
07:00	07:00	07:00	07:00
07:30	07:30	07:30	07:30
08:00	08:00	08:00	08:00
08:30	08:30	08:30	08:30
09:00	09:00	09:00	09:00
09:30	09:30	09:30	09:30
10:00	10:00	10:00	10:00
10:30	10:30	10:30	10:30
11:00	11:00	11:00	11:00
11:30	11:30	11:30	11:30
12:00	12:00	12:00	12:00
12:30	12:30	12:30	12:30
13:00	13:00	13:00	13:00
13:30	13:30	13:30	13:30
14:00	14:00	14:00	14:00
14:30	14:30	14:30	14:30
15:00	15:00	15:00	15:00
15:30	15:30	15:30	15:30
16:00	16:00	16:00	16:00
16:30	16:30	16:30	16:30
17:00	17:00	17:00	17:00
17:30	17:30	17:30	17:30
18:00	18:00	18:00	18:00
18:30	18:30	18:30	18:30
19:00	19:00	19:00	19:00
19:30	19:30	19:30	19:30
20:00	20:00	20:00	20:00
20:30	20:30	20:30	20:30
21:00	21:00	21:00	21:00

NOTES

Daily Sales	Follow Ups	Product Launches	Other Marketing
Monday			
Tuesday			
Wednesday			
Thursday			
Friday			
Saturday			
Sunday			

Pink Fizz SOCIAL

Weekly Review

Top Ideas of the Week

Useful Links and Resources

Ideas For Future Posts

Total New Followers

Checklist

- [ ] REVIEWED YOUR INSIGHTS
- [ ] LIVE/VIDEO/REELS - AT LEAST TWICE
- [ ] REVIEWED YOUR GOALS
- [ ] VISIBLE IN THE 5 GROUPS FOR YOUR IDEAL CUSTOMER
- [ ] COMPLETED SOME PERSONAL DEVELOPMENT
- [ ] RESPONDED TO COMMENTS AND MESSAGES
- [ ] CONNECTED/NETWORKED WITH NEW PEOPLE
- [ ] RESPONDED TO COMMENTS AND MESSAGES
- [ ] FOLLOWED UP LEADS
- [ ] CHECK IN WITH PREVIOUS CUSTOMERS

Weekly Insights

Did you have that lightbulb moment?

My Notes

Weekly Content Planner

Week Commencing

_____

	Monday	Tuesday	Wednesday
Facebook	Posted ☐	Posted ☐	Posted ☐
Twitter	Posted ☐	Posted ☐	Posted ☐
Instagram	Posted ☐	Posted ☐	Posted ☐
LinkedIn	Posted ☐	Posted ☐	Posted ☐
Pinterest	Posted ☐	Posted ☐	Posted ☐
TikTok	Posted ☐	Posted ☐	Posted ☐
Snapchat	Posted ☐	Posted ☐	Posted ☐
Email	Posted ☐	Posted ☐	Posted ☐

Weekly Content Planner

Thursday	Friday	Saturday	Sunday
Posted ☐	Posted ☐	Posted ☐	Posted ☐
Posted ☐	Posted ☐	Posted ☐	Posted ☐
Posted ☐	Posted ☐	Posted ☐	Posted ☐
Posted ☐	Posted ☐	Posted ☐	Posted ☐
Posted ☐	Posted ☐	Posted ☐	Posted ☐
Posted ☐	Posted ☐	Posted ☐	Posted ☐
Posted ☐	Posted ☐	Posted ☐	Posted ☐
Posted ☐	Posted ☐	Posted ☐	Posted ☐

Month: _____

This Week's Priorities
1.
2.
3.
4.
5.

Work To Do List
1.
2.
3.
4.
5.

Personal To Do List
1.
2.
3.
4.
5.

5 Wins
1.
2.
3.
4.
5.

	Monday	Tuesday	Wednesday
Today's Affirmation / Quote			
Today's Goal			
06:00			
06:30			
07:00			
07:30			
08:00			
08:30			
09:00			
09:30			
10:00			
10:30			
11:00			
11:30			
12:00			
12:30			
13:00			
13:30			
14:00			
14:30			
15:00			
15:30			
16:00			
16:30			
17:00			
17:30			
18:00			
18:30			
19:00			
19:30			
20:00			
20:30			
21:00			

NOTES

Post Ideas	Video/Vlogging Ideas	Where I'm Networking	Blogging Ideas

Pink Fizz Social

THURSDAY		FRIDAY		SATURDAY		SUNDAY	
Today's Affirmation / Quote		Today's Affirmation / Quote		Today's Affirmation / Quote		Today's Affirmation / Quote	
Today's Goal		Today's Goal		Today's Goal		Today's Goal	
06:00		06:00		06:00		06:00	
06:30		06:30		06:30		06:30	
07:00		07:00		07:00		07:00	
07:30		07:30		07:30		07:30	
08:00		08:00		08:00		08:00	
08:30		08:30		08:30		08:30	
09:00		09:00		09:00		09:00	
09:30		09:30		09:30		09:30	
10:00		10:00		10:00		10:00	
10:30		10:30		10:30		10:30	
11:00		11:00		11:00		11:00	
11:30		11:30		11:30		11:30	
12:00		12:00		12:00		12:00	
12:30		12:30		12:30		12:30	
13:00		13:00		13:00		13:00	
13:30		13:30		13:30		13:30	
14:00		14:00		14:00		14:00	
14:30		14:30		14:30		14:30	
15:00		15:00		15:00		15:00	
15:30		15:30		15:30		15:30	
16:00		16:00		16:00		16:00	
16:30		16:30		16:30		16:30	
17:00		17:00		17:00		17:00	
17:30		17:30		17:30		17:30	
18:00		18:00		18:00		18:00	
18:30		18:30		18:30		18:30	
19:00		19:00		19:00		19:00	
19:30		19:30		19:30		19:30	
20:00		20:00		20:00		20:00	
20:30		20:30		20:30		20:30	
21:00		21:00		21:00		21:00	

NOTES

Daily Sales

Monday	
Tuesday	
Wednesday	
Thursday	
Friday	
Saturday	
Sunday	

Follow Ups

Product Launches

Other Marketing

Pink Fizz SOCIAL

Weekly Review

Top Ideas of the Week

Useful Links and Resources

Ideas For Future Posts

Total New Followers

Checklist

- Reviewed your insights
- Live/Video/Reels - at least twice
- Reviewed your goals
- Visible in the 5 groups for your ideal customer
- Completed some personal development
- Responded to comments and messages
- Connected/Networked with new people
- Responded to comments and messages
- Followed up leads
- Check in with previous customers

Weekly Insights

Did you have that lightbulb moment?

My Notes

Weekly Content Planner

Week Commencing
_____

	Monday	Tuesday	Wednesday
Facebook	Posted ☐	Posted ☐	Posted ☐
Twitter	Posted ☐	Posted ☐	Posted ☐
Instagram	Posted ☐	Posted ☐	Posted ☐
LinkedIn	Posted ☐	Posted ☐	Posted ☐
Pinterest	Posted ☐	Posted ☐	Posted ☐
TikTok	Posted ☐	Posted ☐	Posted ☐
Snapchat	Posted ☐	Posted ☐	Posted ☐
Email	Posted ☐	Posted ☐	Posted ☐

Weekly Content Planner

Thursday	Friday	Saturday	Sunday
Posted	Posted	Posted	Posted
Posted	Posted	Posted	Posted
Posted	Posted	Posted	Posted
Posted	Posted	Posted	Posted
Posted	Posted	Posted	Posted
Posted	Posted	Posted	Posted
Posted	Posted	Posted	Posted
Posted	Posted	Posted	Posted

Month: _____

This Week's Priorities

| 1 |
| 2 |
| 3 |
| 4 |
| 5 |

Work To Do List

| 1 |
| 2 |
| 3 |
| 4 |
| 5 |

Personal To Do List

| 1 |
| 2 |
| 3 |
| 4 |
| 5 |

5 Wins

| 1 |
| 2 |
| 3 |
| 4 |
| 5 |

	Monday		Tuesday		Wednesday
Today's Affirmation / Quote		Today's Affirmation / Quote		Today's Affirmation / Quote	
Today's Goal		Today's Goal		Today's Goal	

Monday	Tuesday	Wednesday
06:00	06:00	06:00
06:30	06:30	06:30
07:00	07:00	07:00
07:30	07:30	07:30
08:00	08:00	08:00
08:30	08:30	08:30
09:00	09:00	09:00
09:30	09:30	09:30
10:00	10:00	10:00
10:30	10:30	10:30
11:00	11:00	11:00
11:30	11:30	11:30
12:00	12:00	12:00
12:30	12:30	12:30
13:00	13:00	13:00
13:30	13:30	13:30
14:00	14:00	14:00
14:30	14:30	14:30
15:00	15:00	15:00
15:30	15:30	15:30
16:00	16:00	16:00
16:30	16:30	16:30
17:00	17:00	17:00
17:30	17:30	17:30
18:00	18:00	18:00
18:30	18:30	18:30
19:00	19:00	19:00
19:30	19:30	19:30
20:00	20:00	20:00
20:30	20:30	20:30
21:00	21:00	21:00

NOTES

_____

Post Ideas	Video/Vlogging Ideas	Where I'm Networking	Blogging Ideas

Pink Fizz Social

	THURSDAY		FRIDAY		SATURDAY		SUNDAY
Today's Affirmation / Quote		Today's Affirmation / Quote		Today's Affirmation / Quote		Today's Affirmation / Quote	
Today's Goal		Today's Goal		Today's Goal		Today's Goal	
06:00		06:00		06:00		06:00	
06:30		06:30		06:30		06:30	
07:00		07:00		07:00		07:00	
07:30		07:30		07:30		07:30	
08:00		08:00		08:00		08:00	
08:30		08:30		08:30		08:30	
09:00		09:00		09:00		09:00	
09:30		09:30		09:30		09:30	
10:00		10:00		10:00		10:00	
10:30		10:30		10:30		10:30	
11:00		11:00		11:00		11:00	
11:30		11:30		11:30		11:30	
12:00		12:00		12:00		12:00	
12:30		12:30		12:30		12:30	
13:00		13:00		13:00		13:00	
13:30		13:30		13:30		13:30	
14:00		14:00		14:00		14:00	
14:30		14:30		14:30		14:30	
15:00		15:00		15:00		15:00	
15:30		15:30		15:30		15:30	
16:00		16:00		16:00		16:00	
16:30		16:30		16:30		16:30	
17:00		17:00		17:00		17:00	
17:30		17:30		17:30		17:30	
18:00		18:00		18:00		18:00	
18:30		18:30		18:30		18:30	
19:00		19:00		19:00		19:00	
19:30		19:30		19:30		19:30	
20:00		20:00		20:00		20:00	
20:30		20:30		20:30		20:30	
21:00		21:00		21:00		21:00	

NOTES

Daily Sales

- Monday
- Tuesday
- Wednesday
- Thursday
- Friday
- Saturday
- Sunday

Follow Ups

Product Launches

Other Marketing

Pink Fizz SOCIAL

Weekly Review

Top Ideas of the Week

Useful Links and Resources

Ideas For Future Posts

Total New Followers

Checklist

- Reviewed your insights
- Live/Video/Reels - at least twice
- Reviewed your goals
- Visible in the 5 groups for your ideal customer
- Completed some personal development
- Responded to comments and messages
- Connected/networked with new people
- Responded to comments and messages
- Followed up leads
- Check in with previous customers

Weekly Insights

Did you have that lightbulb moment?

My Notes

4 Weekly Reflection

Did I Achieve My Main Focus? _____ If Not Why? _____

_____

What Earnings Did You Reach? _____ Did You Reach Your Goal? _____

How Do I Feel About My Progress

3 Goals I Can Improve On

Lessons Learnt Insights Gained

3 Skills To Improve On

Which Platform Gave Most Visibility

List 5 Types of Post with the Most Engagement

4 Weekly Goals

Month: _____

What Is My Main Focus: _____

What Do I Want To Earn: _____

My 5 Top Goals

When I Feel Like Giving Up I Tell Myself...

Goal: _____
Action Steps:

Deadline: _____

Goal: _____
Action Steps:

Deadline: _____

Goal: _____
Action Steps:

Deadline: _____

Goal: _____
Action Steps:

Deadline: _____

Goal: _____
Action Steps:

Deadline: _____

Weekly Content Planner

Week Commencing
_____

	Monday	Tuesday	Wednesday
Facebook	Posted ☐	Posted ☐	Posted ☐
Twitter	Posted ☐	Posted ☐	Posted ☐
Instagram	Posted ☐	Posted ☐	Posted ☐
LinkedIn	Posted ☐	Posted ☐	Posted ☐
Pinterest	Posted ☐	Posted ☐	Posted ☐
TikTok	Posted ☐	Posted ☐	Posted ☐
Snapchat	Posted ☐	Posted ☐	Posted ☐
Email	Posted ☐	Posted ☐	Posted ☐

Weekly Content Planner

Thursday	Friday	Saturday	Sunday
Posted	Posted	Posted	Posted
Posted	Posted	Posted	Posted
Posted	Posted	Posted	Posted
Posted	Posted	Posted	Posted
Posted	Posted	Posted	Posted
Posted	Posted	Posted	Posted
Posted	Posted	Posted	Posted
Posted	Posted	Posted	Posted

MONTH: _____

THIS WEEK'S PRIORITIES

| 1 |
| 2 |
| 3 |
| 4 |
| 5 |

WORK TO DO LIST

| 1 |
| 2 |
| 3 |
| 4 |
| 5 |

PERSONAL TO DO LIST

| 1 |
| 2 |
| 3 |
| 4 |
| 5 |

5 WINS

| 1 |
| 2 |
| 3 |
| 4 |
| 5 |

	MONDAY	TUESDAY	WEDNESDAY
Today's Affirmation / Quote			
Today's Goal			
06:00			
06:30			
07:00			
07:30			
08:00			
08:30			
09:00			
09:30			
10:00			
10:30			
11:00			
11:30			
12:00			
12:30			
13:00			
13:30			
14:00			
14:30			
15:00			
15:30			
16:00			
16:30			
17:00			
17:30			
18:00			
18:30			
19:00			
19:30			
20:00			
20:30			
21:00			

NOTES

POST IDEAS	VIDEO/VLOGGING IDEAS	WHERE I'M NETWORKING	BLOGGING IDEAS

Pink Fizz SOCIAL

THURSDAY	FRIDAY	SATURDAY	SUNDAY
TODAY'S AFFIRMATION / QUOTE	TODAY'S AFFIRMATION / QUOTE	TODAY'S AFFIRMATION / QUOTE	TODAY'S AFFIRMATION / QUOTE
TODAY'S GOAL	TODAY'S GOAL	TODAY'S GOAL	TODAY'S GOAL
06:00	06:00	06:00	06:00
06:30	06:30	06:30	06:30
07:00	07:00	07:00	07:00
07:30	07:30	07:30	07:30
08:00	08:00	08:00	08:00
08:30	08:30	08:30	08:30
09:00	09:00	09:00	09:00
09:30	09:30	09:30	09:30
10:00	10:00	10:00	10:00
10:30	10:30	10:30	10:30
11:00	11:00	11:00	11:00
11:30	11:30	11:30	11:30
12:00	12:00	12:00	12:00
12:30	12:30	12:30	12:30
13:00	13:00	13:00	13:00
13:30	13:30	13:30	13:30
14:00	14:00	14:00	14:00
14:30	14:30	14:30	14:30
15:00	15:00	15:00	15:00
15:30	15:30	15:30	15:30
16:00	16:00	16:00	16:00
16:30	16:30	16:30	16:30
17:00	17:00	17:00	17:00
17:30	17:30	17:30	17:30
18:00	18:00	18:00	18:00
18:30	18:30	18:30	18:30
19:00	19:00	19:00	19:00
19:30	19:30	19:30	19:30
20:00	20:00	20:00	20:00
20:30	20:30	20:30	20:30
21:00	21:00	21:00	21:00

NOTES

DAILY SALES

- MONDAY
- TUESDAY
- WEDNESDAY
- THURSDAY
- FRIDAY
- SATURDAY
- SUNDAY

FOLLOW UPS

PRODUCT LAUNCHES

OTHER MARKETING

Pink Fizz SOCIAL

Weekly Review

Top Ideas of the Week

Useful Links and Resources

Ideas For Future Posts

Total New Followers

Checklist

- Reviewed your insights
- Live/Video/Reels - at least twice
- Reviewed your goals
- Visible in the 5 groups for your ideal customer
- Completed some personal development
- Responded to comments and messages
- Connected/Networked with new people
- Responded to comments and messages
- Followed up leads
- Check in with previous customers

Weekly Insights

Did you have that lightbulb moment?

My Notes

Weekly Content Planner

Week Commencing
_____

	Monday	Tuesday	Wednesday
Facebook	Posted ☐	Posted ☐	Posted ☐
Twitter	Posted ☐	Posted ☐	Posted ☐
Instagram	Posted ☐	Posted ☐	Posted ☐
LinkedIn	Posted ☐	Posted ☐	Posted ☐
Pinterest	Posted ☐	Posted ☐	Posted ☐
TikTok	Posted ☐	Posted ☐	Posted ☐
Snapchat	Posted ☐	Posted ☐	Posted ☐
Email	Posted ☐	Posted ☐	Posted ☐

Weekly Content Planner

Thursday	Friday	Saturday	Sunday
Posted ☐	Posted ☐	Posted ☐	Posted ☐
Posted ☐	Posted ☐	Posted ☐	Posted ☐
Posted ☐	Posted ☐	Posted ☐	Posted ☐
Posted ☐	Posted ☐	Posted ☐	Posted ☐
Posted ☐	Posted ☐	Posted ☐	Posted ☐
Posted ☐	Posted ☐	Posted ☐	Posted ☐
Posted ☐	Posted ☐	Posted ☐	Posted ☐
Posted ☐	Posted ☐	Posted ☐	Posted ☐

MONTH: _____

THIS WEEK'S PRIORITIES

1.
2.
3.
4.
5.

WORK TO DO LIST

1.
2.
3.
4.
5.

PERSONAL TO DO LIST

1.
2.
3.
4.
5.

5 WINS

1.
2.
3.
4.
5.

	MONDAY	TUESDAY	WEDNESDAY
Today's Affirmation / Quote			
Today's Goal			
06:00			
06:30			
07:00			
07:30			
08:00			
08:30			
09:00			
09:30			
10:00			
10:30			
11:00			
11:30			
12:00			
12:30			
13:00			
13:30			
14:00			
14:30			
15:00			
15:30			
16:00			
16:30			
17:00			
17:30			
18:00			
18:30			
19:00			
19:30			
20:00			
20:30			
21:00			

NOTES

POST IDEAS	VIDEO/VLOGGING IDEAS	WHERE I'M NETWORKING	BLOGGING IDEAS

Pink Fizz Social

THURSDAY	FRIDAY	SATURDAY	SUNDAY
TODAY'S AFFIRMATION / QUOTE	TODAY'S AFFIRMATION / QUOTE	TODAY'S AFFIRMATION / QUOTE	TODAY'S AFFIRMATION / QUOTE
TODAY'S GOAL	TODAY'S GOAL	TODAY'S GOAL	TODAY'S GOAL
06:00	06:00	06:00	06:00
06:30	06:30	06:30	06:30
07:00	07:00	07:00	07:00
07:30	07:30	07:30	07:30
08:00	08:00	08:00	08:00
08:30	08:30	08:30	08:30
09:00	09:00	09:00	09:00
09:30	09:30	09:30	09:30
10:00	10:00	10:00	10:00
10:30	10:30	10:30	10:30
11:00	11:00	11:00	11:00
11:30	11:30	11:30	11:30
12:00	12:00	12:00	12:00
12:30	12:30	12:30	12:30
13:00	13:00	13:00	13:00
13:30	13:30	13:30	13:30
14:00	14:00	14:00	14:00
14:30	14:30	14:30	14:30
15:00	15:00	15:00	15:00
15:30	15:30	15:30	15:30
16:00	16:00	16:00	16:00
16:30	16:30	16:30	16:30
17:00	17:00	17:00	17:00
17:30	17:30	17:30	17:30
18:00	18:00	18:00	18:00
18:30	18:30	18:30	18:30
19:00	19:00	19:00	19:00
19:30	19:30	19:30	19:30
20:00	20:00	20:00	20:00
20:30	20:30	20:30	20:30
21:00	21:00	21:00	21:00

NOTES

DAILY SALES

- MONDAY
- TUESDAY
- WEDNESDAY
- THURSDAY
- FRIDAY
- SATURDAY
- SUNDAY

FOLLOW UPS

PRODUCT LAUNCHES

OTHER MARKETING

Pink Fizz SOCIAL

Weekly Review

Top Ideas of the Week

Useful Links and Resources

Ideas For Future Posts

Total New Followers

Checklist

- Reviewed your insights
- Live/Video/Reels - at least twice
- Reviewed your goals
- Visible in the 5 groups for your ideal customer
- Completed some personal development
- Responded to comments and messages
- Connected/Networked with new people
- Responded to comments and messages
- Followed up leads
- Check in with previous customers

Weekly Insights

Did you have that lightbulb moment?

My Notes

Weekly Content Planner

Week Commencing
_____

	Monday	Tuesday	Wednesday
Facebook	Posted ☐	Posted ☐	Posted ☐
Twitter	Posted ☐	Posted ☐	Posted ☐
Instagram	Posted ☐	Posted ☐	Posted ☐
LinkedIn	Posted ☐	Posted ☐	Posted ☐
Pinterest	Posted ☐	Posted ☐	Posted ☐
TikTok	Posted ☐	Posted ☐	Posted ☐
Snapchat	Posted ☐	Posted ☐	Posted ☐
Email	Posted ☐	Posted ☐	Posted ☐

Weekly Content Planner

Thursday	Friday	Saturday	Sunday
Posted	Posted	Posted	Posted
Posted	Posted	Posted	Posted
Posted	Posted	Posted	Posted
Posted	Posted	Posted	Posted
Posted	Posted	Posted	Posted
Posted	Posted	Posted	Posted
Posted	Posted	Posted	Posted
Posted	Posted	Posted	Posted

MONTH: _____

THIS WEEK'S PRIORITIES

1	
2	
3	
4	
5	

WORK TO DO LIST

1	
2	
3	
4	
5	

PERSONAL TO DO LIST

1	
2	
3	
4	
5	

5 WINS

1	
2	
3	
4	
5	

	MONDAY		TUESDAY		WEDNESDAY	
Today's Affirmation / Quote		Today's Affirmation / Quote		Today's Affirmation / Quote		
Today's Goal		Today's Goal		Today's Goal		
06:00		06:00		06:00		
06:30		06:30		06:30		
07:00		07:00		07:00		
07:30		07:30		07:30		
08:00		08:00		08:00		
08:30		08:30		08:30		
09:00		09:00		09:00		
09:30		09:30		09:30		
10:00		10:00		10:00		
10:30		10:30		10:30		
11:00		11:00		11:00		
11:30		11:30		11:30		
12:00		12:00		12:00		
12:30		12:30		12:30		
13:00		13:00		13:00		
13:30		13:30		13:30		
14:00		14:00		14:00		
14:30		14:30		14:30		
15:00		15:00		15:00		
15:30		15:30		15:30		
16:00		16:00		16:00		
16:30		16:30		16:30		
17:00		17:00		17:00		
17:30		17:30		17:30		
18:00		18:00		18:00		
18:30		18:30		18:30		
19:00		19:00		19:00		
19:30		19:30		19:30		
20:00		20:00		20:00		
20:30		20:30		20:30		
21:00		21:00		21:00		

NOTES

_____

POST IDEAS	VIDEO/VLOGGING IDEAS	WHERE I'M NETWORKING	BLOGGING IDEAS

Pink Fizz SOCIAL

THURSDAY	FRIDAY	SATURDAY	SUNDAY
Today's Affirmation / Quote	Today's Affirmation / Quote	Today's Affirmation / Quote	Today's Affirmation / Quote
Today's Goal	Today's Goal	Today's Goal	Today's Goal
06:00	06:00	06:00	06:00
06:30	06:30	06:30	06:30
07:00	07:00	07:00	07:00
07:30	07:30	07:30	07:30
08:00	08:00	08:00	08:00
08:30	08:30	08:30	08:30
09:00	09:00	09:00	09:00
09:30	09:30	09:30	09:30
10:00	10:00	10:00	10:00
10:30	10:30	10:30	10:30
11:00	11:00	11:00	11:00
11:30	11:30	11:30	11:30
12:00	12:00	12:00	12:00
12:30	12:30	12:30	12:30
13:00	13:00	13:00	13:00
13:30	13:30	13:30	13:30
14:00	14:00	14:00	14:00
14:30	14:30	14:30	14:30
15:00	15:00	15:00	15:00
15:30	15:30	15:30	15:30
16:00	16:00	16:00	16:00
16:30	16:30	16:30	16:30
17:00	17:00	17:00	17:00
17:30	17:30	17:30	17:30
18:00	18:00	18:00	18:00
18:30	18:30	18:30	18:30
19:00	19:00	19:00	19:00
19:30	19:30	19:30	19:30
20:00	20:00	20:00	20:00
20:30	20:30	20:30	20:30
21:00	21:00	21:00	21:00

NOTES

Daily Sales	Follow Ups	Product Launches	Other Marketing
Monday			
Tuesday			
Wednesday			
Thursday			
Friday			
Saturday			
Sunday			

Pink Fizz SOCIAL

Weekly Review

Top Ideas of the Week

Useful Links and Resources

Ideas For Future Posts

Total New Followers

Checklist

- Reviewed your insights
- Live/Video/Reels - at least twice
- Reviewed your goals
- Visible in the 5 groups for your ideal customer
- Completed some personal development
- Responded to comments and messages
- Connected/networked with new people
- Responded to comments and messages
- Followed up leads
- Check in with previous customers

Weekly Insights

Did you have that lightbulb moment?

My Notes

Weekly Content Planner

Week Commencing
_____

	Monday	Tuesday	Wednesday
Facebook	Posted ☐	Posted ☐	Posted ☐
Twitter	Posted ☐	Posted ☐	Posted ☐
Instagram	Posted ☐	Posted ☐	Posted ☐
LinkedIn	Posted ☐	Posted ☐	Posted ☐
Pinterest	Posted ☐	Posted ☐	Posted ☐
TikTok	Posted ☐	Posted ☐	Posted ☐
Snapchat	Posted ☐	Posted ☐	Posted ☐
Email	Posted ☐	Posted ☐	Posted ☐

Weekly Content Planner

Thursday	Friday	Saturday	Sunday
Posted	Posted	Posted	Posted
Posted	Posted	Posted	Posted
Posted	Posted	Posted	Posted
Posted	Posted	Posted	Posted
Posted	Posted	Posted	Posted
Posted	Posted	Posted	Posted
Posted	Posted	Posted	Posted
Posted	Posted	Posted	Posted

MONTH: _____

THIS WEEK'S PRIORITIES
1	
2	
3	
4	
5	

WORK TO DO LIST
1	
2	
3	
4	
5	

PERSONAL TO DO LIST
1	
2	
3	
4	
5	

5 WINS
1	
2	
3	
4	
5	

MONDAY | TUESDAY | WEDNESDAY

Time	Monday	Tuesday	Wednesday
Today's Affirmation / Quote			
Today's Goal			
06:00			
06:30			
07:00			
07:30			
08:00			
08:30			
09:00			
09:30			
10:00			
10:30			
11:00			
11:30			
12:00			
12:30			
13:00			
13:30			
14:00			
14:30			
15:00			
15:30			
16:00			
16:30			
17:00			
17:30			
18:00			
18:30			
19:00			
19:30			
20:00			
20:30			
21:00			

NOTES

POST IDEAS	VIDEO/VLOGGING IDEAS	WHERE I'M NETWORKING	BLOGGING IDEAS

Pink Fizz SOCIAL

THURSDAY | FRIDAY | SATURDAY | SUNDAY

	Thursday		Friday		Saturday		Sunday
Today's Affirmation / Quote		Today's Affirmation / Quote		Today's Affirmation / Quote		Today's Affirmation / Quote	
Today's Goal		Today's Goal		Today's Goal		Today's Goal	
06:00		06:00		06:00		06:00	
06:30		06:30		06:30		06:30	
07:00		07:00		07:00		07:00	
07:30		07:30		07:30		07:30	
08:00		08:00		08:00		08:00	
08:30		08:30		08:30		08:30	
09:00		09:00		09:00		09:00	
09:30		09:30		09:30		09:30	
10:00		10:00		10:00		10:00	
10:30		10:30		10:30		10:30	
11:00		11:00		11:00		11:00	
11:30		11:30		11:30		11:30	
12:00		12:00		12:00		12:00	
12:30		12:30		12:30		12:30	
13:00		13:00		13:00		13:00	
13:30		13:30		13:30		13:30	
14:00		14:00		14:00		14:00	
14:30		14:30		14:30		14:30	
15:00		15:00		15:00		15:00	
15:30		15:30		15:30		15:30	
16:00		16:00		16:00		16:00	
16:30		16:30		16:30		16:30	
17:00		17:00		17:00		17:00	
17:30		17:30		17:30		17:30	
18:00		18:00		18:00		18:00	
18:30		18:30		18:30		18:30	
19:00		19:00		19:00		19:00	
19:30		19:30		19:30		19:30	
20:00		20:00		20:00		20:00	
20:30		20:30		20:30		20:30	
21:00		21:00		21:00		21:00	

NOTES

Daily Sales	Follow Ups	Product Launches	Other Marketing
Monday			
Tuesday			
Wednesday			
Thursday			
Friday			
Saturday			
Sunday			

Pink Fizz SOCIAL

Weekly Review

Top Ideas of the Week

Useful Links and Resources

Ideas For Future Posts

Total New Followers

Checklist

- Reviewed your insights
- Live/Video/Reels - at least twice
- Reviewed your goals
- Visible in the 5 groups for your ideal customer
- Completed some personal development
- Responded to comments and messages
- Connected/networked with new people
- Responded to comments and messages
- Followed up leads
- Check in with previous customers

Weekly Insights

Did you have that lightbulb moment?

My Notes

4 Weekly Reflection

Did I Achieve My Main Focus? _____   If Not Why? _____
_____

What Earnings Did You Reach? _____   Did You Reach Your Goal? _____

How Do I Feel About My Progress

3 Goals I Can Improve On

Lessons Learnt Insights Gained

3 Skills To Improve On

Which Platform Gave Most Visibility

List 5 Types of Post with the Most Engagement

4 Weekly Goals   Month: _____

What Is My Main Focus: _____

What Do I Want To Earn: _____

My 5 Top Goals

When I Feel Like Giving Up I Tell Myself...

Goal: _____
Action Steps:

Deadline: _____

Goal: _____
Action Steps:

Deadline: _____

Goal: _____
Action Steps:

Deadline: _____

Goal: _____
Action Steps:

Deadline: _____

Goal: _____
Action Steps:

Deadline: _____

Weekly Content Planner

Week Commencing
_____

	Monday	Tuesday	Wednesday
Facebook	Posted ☐	Posted ☐	Posted ☐
Twitter	Posted ☐	Posted ☐	Posted ☐
Instagram	Posted ☐	Posted ☐	Posted ☐
LinkedIn	Posted ☐	Posted ☐	Posted ☐
Pinterest	Posted ☐	Posted ☐	Posted ☐
TikTok	Posted ☐	Posted ☐	Posted ☐
Snapchat	Posted ☐	Posted ☐	Posted ☐
Email	Posted ☐	Posted ☐	Posted ☐

Weekly Content Planner

Thursday	Friday	Saturday	Sunday
Posted ☐	Posted ☐	Posted ☐	Posted ☐
Posted ☐	Posted ☐	Posted ☐	Posted ☐
Posted ☐	Posted ☐	Posted ☐	Posted ☐
Posted ☐	Posted ☐	Posted ☐	Posted ☐
Posted ☐	Posted ☐	Posted ☐	Posted ☐
Posted ☐	Posted ☐	Posted ☐	Posted ☐
Posted ☐	Posted ☐	Posted ☐	Posted ☐
Posted ☐	Posted ☐	Posted ☐	Posted ☐

MONTH: _____

This Week's Priorities

| 1 |
| 2 |
| 3 |
| 4 |
| 5 |

Work To Do List

| 1 |
| 2 |
| 3 |
| 4 |
| 5 |

Personal To Do List

| 1 |
| 2 |
| 3 |
| 4 |
| 5 |

5 Wins

| 1 |
| 2 |
| 3 |
| 4 |
| 5 |

	MONDAY	TUESDAY	WEDNESDAY
Today's Affirmation / Quote			
Today's Goal			
06:00			
06:30			
07:00			
07:30			
08:00			
08:30			
09:00			
09:30			
10:00			
10:30			
11:00			
11:30			
12:00			
12:30			
13:00			
13:30			
14:00			
14:30			
15:00			
15:30			
16:00			
16:30			
17:00			
17:30			
18:00			
18:30			
19:00			
19:30			
20:00			
20:30			
21:00			

NOTES

Post Ideas	Video/Vlogging Ideas	Where I'm Networking	Blogging Ideas

Pink Fizz SOCIAL

THURSDAY	FRIDAY	SATURDAY	SUNDAY
Today's Affirmation / Quote	Today's Affirmation / Quote	Today's Affirmation / Quote	Today's Affirmation / Quote
Today's Goal	Today's Goal	Today's Goal	Today's Goal

Thursday	Friday	Saturday	Sunday
06:00	06:00	06:00	06:00
06:30	06:30	06:30	06:30
07:00	07:00	07:00	07:00
07:30	07:30	07:30	07:30
08:00	08:00	08:00	08:00
08:30	08:30	08:30	08:30
09:00	09:00	09:00	09:00
09:30	09:30	09:30	09:30
10:00	10:00	10:00	10:00
10:30	10:30	10:30	10:30
11:00	11:00	11:00	11:00
11:30	11:30	11:30	11:30
12:00	12:00	12:00	12:00
12:30	12:30	12:30	12:30
13:00	13:00	13:00	13:00
13:30	13:30	13:30	13:30
14:00	14:00	14:00	14:00
14:30	14:30	14:30	14:30
15:00	15:00	15:00	15:00
15:30	15:30	15:30	15:30
16:00	16:00	16:00	16:00
16:30	16:30	16:30	16:30
17:00	17:00	17:00	17:00
17:30	17:30	17:30	17:30
18:00	18:00	18:00	18:00
18:30	18:30	18:30	18:30
19:00	19:00	19:00	19:00
19:30	19:30	19:30	19:30
20:00	20:00	20:00	20:00
20:30	20:30	20:30	20:30
21:00	21:00	21:00	21:00

NOTES

Daily Sales	Follow Ups	Product Launches	Other Marketing
Monday			
Tuesday			
Wednesday			
Thursday			
Friday			
Saturday			
Sunday			

Pink Fizz SOCIAL

Weekly Review

Top Ideas of the Week

Useful Links and Resources

Ideas For Future Posts

Total New Followers

Checklist

- Reviewed your insights
- Live/Video/Reels - at least twice
- Reviewed your goals
- Visible in the 5 groups for your ideal customer
- Completed some personal development
- Responded to comments and messages
- Connected/networked with new people
- Responded to comments and messages
- Followed up leads
- Check in with previous customers

Weekly Insights

Did you have that lightbulb moment?

My Notes

Weekly Content Planner

Week Commencing
_____

	MONDAY	TUESDAY	WEDNESDAY
Facebook	Posted ☐	Posted ☐	Posted ☐
Twitter	Posted ☐	Posted ☐	Posted ☐
Instagram	Posted ☐	Posted ☐	Posted ☐
LinkedIn	Posted ☐	Posted ☐	Posted ☐
Pinterest	Posted ☐	Posted ☐	Posted ☐
TikTok	Posted ☐	Posted ☐	Posted ☐
Snapchat	Posted ☐	Posted ☐	Posted ☐
Email	Posted ☐	Posted ☐	Posted ☐

Weekly Content Planner

Thursday	Friday	Saturday	Sunday
Posted	Posted	Posted	Posted
Posted	Posted	Posted	Posted
Posted	Posted	Posted	Posted
Posted	Posted	Posted	Posted
Posted	Posted	Posted	Posted
Posted	Posted	Posted	Posted
Posted	Posted	Posted	Posted
Posted	Posted	Posted	Posted

Month: _____

This Week's Priorities

1	
2	
3	
4	
5	

Work To Do List

1	
2	
3	
4	
5	

Personal To Do List

1	
2	
3	
4	
5	

5 Wins

1	
2	
3	
4	
5	

	Monday	Tuesday	Wednesday
Today's Affirmation / Quote			
Today's Goal			
06:00			
06:30			
07:00			
07:30			
08:00			
08:30			
09:00			
09:30			
10:00			
10:30			
11:00			
11:30			
12:00			
12:30			
13:00			
13:30			
14:00			
14:30			
15:00			
15:30			
16:00			
16:30			
17:00			
17:30			
18:00			
18:30			
19:00			
19:30			
20:00			
20:30			
21:00			

NOTES

Post Ideas | Video/Vlogging Ideas | Where I'm Networking | Blogging Ideas

Pink Fizz Social

	THURSDAY		FRIDAY		SATURDAY		SUNDAY
Today's Affirmation / Quote		Today's Affirmation / Quote		Today's Affirmation / Quote		Today's Affirmation / Quote	
Today's Goal		Today's Goal		Today's Goal		Today's Goal	
06:00		06:00		06:00		06:00	
06:30		06:30		06:30		06:30	
07:00		07:00		07:00		07:00	
07:30		07:30		07:30		07:30	
08:00		08:00		08:00		08:00	
08:30		08:30		08:30		08:30	
09:00		09:00		09:00		09:00	
09:30		09:30		09:30		09:30	
10:00		10:00		10:00		10:00	
10:30		10:30		10:30		10:30	
11:00		11:00		11:00		11:00	
11:30		11:30		11:30		11:30	
12:00		12:00		12:00		12:00	
12:30		12:30		12:30		12:30	
13:00		13:00		13:00		13:00	
13:30		13:30		13:30		13:30	
14:00		14:00		14:00		14:00	
14:30		14:30		14:30		14:30	
15:00		15:00		15:00		15:00	
15:30		15:30		15:30		15:30	
16:00		16:00		16:00		16:00	
16:30		16:30		16:30		16:30	
17:00		17:00		17:00		17:00	
17:30		17:30		17:30		17:30	
18:00		18:00		18:00		18:00	
18:30		18:30		18:30		18:30	
19:00		19:00		19:00		19:00	
19:30		19:30		19:30		19:30	
20:00		20:00		20:00		20:00	
20:30		20:30		20:30		20:30	
21:00		21:00		21:00		21:00	

NOTES

Daily Sales	Follow Ups	Product Launches	Other Marketing
Monday			
Tuesday			
Wednesday			
Thursday			
Friday			
Saturday			
Sunday			

Pink Fizz SOCIAL

Weekly Review

Top Ideas of the Week

Useful Links and Resources

Ideas For Future Posts

Total New Followers

Checklist

- Reviewed your insights
- Live/Video/Reels - at least twice
- Reviewed your goals
- Visible in the 5 groups for your ideal customer
- Completed some personal development
- Responded to comments and messages
- Connected/Networked with new people
- Responded to comments and messages
- Followed up leads
- Check in with previous customers

Weekly Insights

Did you have that lightbulb moment?

My Notes

Weekly Content Planner

Week Commencing
_____

	Monday	Tuesday	Wednesday
Facebook	Posted ☐	Posted ☐	Posted ☐
Twitter	Posted ☐	Posted ☐	Posted ☐
Instagram	Posted ☐	Posted ☐	Posted ☐
LinkedIn	Posted ☐	Posted ☐	Posted ☐
Pinterest	Posted ☐	Posted ☐	Posted ☐
TikTok	Posted ☐	Posted ☐	Posted ☐
Snapchat	Posted ☐	Posted ☐	Posted ☐
Email	Posted ☐	Posted ☐	Posted ☐

Weekly Content Planner

Thursday	Friday	Saturday	Sunday
Posted ☐	Posted ☐	Posted ☐	Posted ☐
Posted ☐	Posted ☐	Posted ☐	Posted ☐
Posted ☐	Posted ☐	Posted ☐	Posted ☐
Posted ☐	Posted ☐	Posted ☐	Posted ☐
Posted ☐	Posted ☐	Posted ☐	Posted ☐
Posted ☐	Posted ☐	Posted ☐	Posted ☐
Posted ☐	Posted ☐	Posted ☐	Posted ☐
Posted ☐	Posted ☐	Posted ☐	Posted ☐

MONTH: _____

THIS WEEK'S PRIORITIES

1	
2	
3	
4	
5	

WORK TO DO LIST

1	
2	
3	
4	
5	

PERSONAL TO DO LIST

1	
2	
3	
4	
5	

5 WINS

1	
2	
3	
4	
5	

	MONDAY		TUESDAY		WEDNESDAY
Today's Affirmation / Quote		Today's Affirmation / Quote		Today's Affirmation / Quote	
Today's Goal		Today's Goal		Today's Goal	
06:00		06:00		06:00	
06:30		06:30		06:30	
07:00		07:00		07:00	
07:30		07:30		07:30	
08:00		08:00		08:00	
08:30		08:30		08:30	
09:00		09:00		09:00	
09:30		09:30		09:30	
10:00		10:00		10:00	
10:30		10:30		10:30	
11:00		11:00		11:00	
11:30		11:30		11:30	
12:00		12:00		12:00	
12:30		12:30		12:30	
13:00		13:00		13:00	
13:30		13:30		13:30	
14:00		14:00		14:00	
14:30		14:30		14:30	
15:00		15:00		15:00	
15:30		15:30		15:30	
16:00		16:00		16:00	
16:30		16:30		16:30	
17:00		17:00		17:00	
17:30		17:30		17:30	
18:00		18:00		18:00	
18:30		18:30		18:30	
19:00		19:00		19:00	
19:30		19:30		19:30	
20:00		20:00		20:00	
20:30		20:30		20:30	
21:00		21:00		21:00	

NOTES

POST IDEAS	VIDEO/VLOGGING IDEAS	WHERE I'M NETWORKING	BLOGGING IDEAS

Pink Fizz SOCIAL

	THURSDAY	FRIDAY	SATURDAY	SUNDAY
Today's Affirmation / Quote				
Today's Goal				
06:00				
06:30				
07:00				
07:30				
08:00				
08:30				
09:00				
09:30				
10:00				
10:30				
11:00				
11:30				
12:00				
12:30				
13:00				
13:30				
14:00				
14:30				
15:00				
15:30				
16:00				
16:30				
17:00				
17:30				
18:00				
18:30				
19:00				
19:30				
20:00				
20:30				
21:00				

NOTES

Daily Sales	Follow Ups	Product Launches	Other Marketing
Monday			
Tuesday			
Wednesday			
Thursday			
Friday			
Saturday			
Sunday			

Pink Fizz SOCIAL

Weekly Review

Top Ideas of the Week

Useful Links and Resources

Ideas For Future Posts

Total New Followers

Checklist

- Reviewed your insights
- Live/Video/Reels - at least twice
- Reviewed your goals
- Visible in the 5 groups for your ideal customer
- Completed some personal development
- Responded to comments and messages
- Connected/Networked with new people
- Responded to comments and messages
- Followed up leads
- Check in with previous customers

Weekly Insights

Did you have that lightbulb moment?

My Notes

Weekly Content Planner

Week Commencing
_____

	Monday	Tuesday	Wednesday
Facebook	Posted ☐	Posted ☐	Posted ☐
Twitter	Posted ☐	Posted ☐	Posted ☐
Instagram	Posted ☐	Posted ☐	Posted ☐
LinkedIn	Posted ☐	Posted ☐	Posted ☐
Pinterest	Posted ☐	Posted ☐	Posted ☐
TikTok	Posted ☐	Posted ☐	Posted ☐
Snapchat	Posted ☐	Posted ☐	Posted ☐
Email	Posted ☐	Posted ☐	Posted ☐

Weekly Content Planner

Thursday	Friday	Saturday	Sunday
Posted ☐	Posted ☐	Posted ☐	Posted ☐
Posted ☐	Posted ☐	Posted ☐	Posted ☐
Posted ☐	Posted ☐	Posted ☐	Posted ☐
Posted ☐	Posted ☐	Posted ☐	Posted ☐
Posted ☐	Posted ☐	Posted ☐	Posted ☐
Posted ☐	Posted ☐	Posted ☐	Posted ☐
Posted ☐	Posted ☐	Posted ☐	Posted ☐
Posted ☐	Posted ☐	Posted ☐	Posted ☐

MONTH: _____

THIS WEEK'S PRIORITIES
1.
2.
3.
4.
5.

WORK TO DO LIST
1.
2.
3.
4.
5.

PERSONAL TO DO LIST
1.
2.
3.
4.
5.

5 WINS
1.
2.
3.
4.
5.

	MONDAY		TUESDAY		WEDNESDAY
Today's Affirmation / Quote		Today's Affirmation / Quote		Today's Affirmation / Quote	
Today's Goal		Today's Goal		Today's Goal	
06:00		06:00		06:00	
06:30		06:30		06:30	
07:00		07:00		07:00	
07:30		07:30		07:30	
08:00		08:00		08:00	
08:30		08:30		08:30	
09:00		09:00		09:00	
09:30		09:30		09:30	
10:00		10:00		10:00	
10:30		10:30		10:30	
11:00		11:00		11:00	
11:30		11:30		11:30	
12:00		12:00		12:00	
12:30		12:30		12:30	
13:00		13:00		13:00	
13:30		13:30		13:30	
14:00		14:00		14:00	
14:30		14:30		14:30	
15:00		15:00		15:00	
15:30		15:30		15:30	
16:00		16:00		16:00	
16:30		16:30		16:30	
17:00		17:00		17:00	
17:30		17:30		17:30	
18:00		18:00		18:00	
18:30		18:30		18:30	
19:00		19:00		19:00	
19:30		19:30		19:30	
20:00		20:00		20:00	
20:30		20:30		20:30	
21:00		21:00		21:00	

NOTES

_____

POST IDEAS	VIDEO/VLOGGING IDEAS	WHERE I'M NETWORKING	BLOGGING IDEAS

Pink Fizz SOCIAL

THURSDAY	FRIDAY	SATURDAY	SUNDAY
Today's Affirmation / Quote	**Today's Affirmation / Quote**	**Today's Affirmation / Quote**	**Today's Affirmation / Quote**
Today's Goal	**Today's Goal**	**Today's Goal**	**Today's Goal**
06:00	06:00	06:00	06:00
06:30	06:30	06:30	06:30
07:00	07:00	07:00	07:00
07:30	07:30	07:30	07:30
08:00	08:00	08:00	08:00
08:30	08:30	08:30	08:30
09:00	09:00	09:00	09:00
09:30	09:30	09:30	09:30
10:00	10:00	10:00	10:00
10:30	10:30	10:30	10:30
11:00	11:00	11:00	11:00
11:30	11:30	11:30	11:30
12:00	12:00	12:00	12:00
12:30	12:30	12:30	12:30
13:00	13:00	13:00	13:00
13:30	13:30	13:30	13:30
14:00	14:00	14:00	14:00
14:30	14:30	14:30	14:30
15:00	15:00	15:00	15:00
15:30	15:30	15:30	15:30
16:00	16:00	16:00	16:00
16:30	16:30	16:30	16:30
17:00	17:00	17:00	17:00
17:30	17:30	17:30	17:30
18:00	18:00	18:00	18:00
18:30	18:30	18:30	18:30
19:00	19:00	19:00	19:00
19:30	19:30	19:30	19:30
20:00	20:00	20:00	20:00
20:30	20:30	20:30	20:30
21:00	21:00	21:00	21:00

NOTES

Daily Sales

- Monday
- Tuesday
- Wednesday
- Thursday
- Friday
- Saturday
- Sunday

Follow Ups

Product Launches

Other Marketing

Pink Fizz Social

Weekly Review

Top Ideas of the Week

Useful Links and Resources

Ideas For Future Posts

Total New Followers

Checklist

- Reviewed your insights
- Live/Video/Reels - at least twice
- Reviewed your goals
- Visible in the 5 groups for your ideal customer
- Completed some personal development
- Responded to comments and messages
- Connected/Networked with new people
- Responded to comments and messages
- Followed up leads
- Check in with previous customers

Weekly Insights

Did you have that lightbulb moment?

My Notes

4 Weekly Reflection

Did I Achieve My Main Focus? _____   If Not Why? _____
_____

What Earnings Did You Reach? _____   Did You Reach Your Goal? _____

How Do I Feel About My Progress

3 Goals I Can Improve On

Lessons Learnt Insights Gained

3 Skills To Improve On

Which Platform Gave Most Visibility

List 5 Types of Post with the Most Engagement

4 Weekly Goals

MONTH: _____

WHAT IS MY MAIN FOCUS: _____

WHAT DO I WANT TO EARN: _____

My 5 Top Goals

When I Feel Like Giving Up I Tell Myself...

GOAL: _____
ACTION STEPS:

DEADLINE: _____

GOAL: _____
ACTION STEPS:

DEADLINE: _____

GOAL: _____
ACTION STEPS:

DEADLINE: _____

GOAL: _____
ACTION STEPS:

DEADLINE: _____

GOAL: _____
ACTION STEPS:

DEADLINE: _____

Weekly Content Planner

Week Commencing
_____

	Monday	Tuesday	Wednesday
Facebook	Posted ☐	Posted ☐	Posted ☐
Twitter	Posted ☐	Posted ☐	Posted ☐
Instagram	Posted ☐	Posted ☐	Posted ☐
LinkedIn	Posted ☐	Posted ☐	Posted ☐
Pinterest	Posted ☐	Posted ☐	Posted ☐
TikTok	Posted ☐	Posted ☐	Posted ☐
Snapchat	Posted ☐	Posted ☐	Posted ☐
Email	Posted ☐	Posted ☐	Posted ☐

Weekly Content Planner

Thursday	Friday	Saturday	Sunday
Posted	Posted	Posted	Posted
Posted	Posted	Posted	Posted
Posted	Posted	Posted	Posted
Posted	Posted	Posted	Posted
Posted	Posted	Posted	Posted
Posted	Posted	Posted	Posted
Posted	Posted	Posted	Posted
Posted	Posted	Posted	Posted

MONTH: _____

THIS WEEK'S PRIORITIES
1.
2.
3.
4.
5.

WORK TO DO LIST
1.
2.
3.
4.
5.

PERSONAL TO DO LIST
1.
2.
3.
4.
5.

5 WINS
1.
2.
3.
4.
5.

MONDAY

Today's Affirmation / Quote

Today's Goal

| 06:00 |
| 06:30 |
| 07:00 |
| 07:30 |
| 08:00 |
| 08:30 |
| 09:00 |
| 09:30 |
| 10:00 |
| 10:30 |
| 11:00 |
| 11:30 |
| 12:00 |
| 12:30 |
| 13:00 |
| 13:30 |
| 14:00 |
| 14:30 |
| 15:00 |
| 15:30 |
| 16:00 |
| 16:30 |
| 17:00 |
| 17:30 |
| 18:00 |
| 18:30 |
| 19:00 |
| 19:30 |
| 20:00 |
| 20:30 |
| 21:00 |

TUESDAY

Today's Affirmation / Quote

Today's Goal

| 06:00 |
| 06:30 |
| 07:00 |
| 07:30 |
| 08:00 |
| 08:30 |
| 09:00 |
| 09:30 |
| 10:00 |
| 10:30 |
| 11:00 |
| 11:30 |
| 12:00 |
| 12:30 |
| 13:00 |
| 13:30 |
| 14:00 |
| 14:30 |
| 15:00 |
| 15:30 |
| 16:00 |
| 16:30 |
| 17:00 |
| 17:30 |
| 18:00 |
| 18:30 |
| 19:00 |
| 19:30 |
| 20:00 |
| 20:30 |
| 21:00 |

WEDNESDAY

Today's Affirmation / Quote

Today's Goal

| 06:00 |
| 06:30 |
| 07:00 |
| 07:30 |
| 08:00 |
| 08:30 |
| 09:00 |
| 09:30 |
| 10:00 |
| 10:30 |
| 11:00 |
| 11:30 |
| 12:00 |
| 12:30 |
| 13:00 |
| 13:30 |
| 14:00 |
| 14:30 |
| 15:00 |
| 15:30 |
| 16:00 |
| 16:30 |
| 17:00 |
| 17:30 |
| 18:00 |
| 18:30 |
| 19:00 |
| 19:30 |
| 20:00 |
| 20:30 |
| 21:00 |

NOTES

POST IDEAS | VIDEO/VLOGGING IDEAS | WHERE I'M NETWORKING | BLOGGING IDEAS

Pink Fizz SOCIAL

THURSDAY	FRIDAY	SATURDAY	SUNDAY
Today's Affirmation / Quote	Today's Affirmation / Quote	Today's Affirmation / Quote	Today's Affirmation / Quote
Today's Goal	Today's Goal	Today's Goal	Today's Goal
06:00	06:00	06:00	06:00
06:30	06:30	06:30	06:30
07:00	07:00	07:00	07:00
07:30	07:30	07:30	07:30
08:00	08:00	08:00	08:00
08:30	08:30	08:30	08:30
09:00	09:00	09:00	09:00
09:30	09:30	09:30	09:30
10:00	10:00	10:00	10:00
10:30	10:30	10:30	10:30
11:00	11:00	11:00	11:00
11:30	11:30	11:30	11:30
12:00	12:00	12:00	12:00
12:30	12:30	12:30	12:30
13:00	13:00	13:00	13:00
13:30	13:30	13:30	13:30
14:00	14:00	14:00	14:00
14:30	14:30	14:30	14:30
15:00	15:00	15:00	15:00
15:30	15:30	15:30	15:30
16:00	16:00	16:00	16:00
16:30	16:30	16:30	16:30
17:00	17:00	17:00	17:00
17:30	17:30	17:30	17:30
18:00	18:00	18:00	18:00
18:30	18:30	18:30	18:30
19:00	19:00	19:00	19:00
19:30	19:30	19:30	19:30
20:00	20:00	20:00	20:00
20:30	20:30	20:30	20:30
21:00	21:00	21:00	21:00

NOTES

Daily Sales	Follow Ups	Product Launches	Other Marketing
Monday			
Tuesday			
Wednesday			
Thursday			
Friday			
Saturday			
Sunday			

Pink Fizz SOCIAL

Weekly Review

Top Ideas of the Week

Useful Links and Resources

Ideas For Future Posts

Total New Followers

Checklist

- REVIEWED YOUR INSIGHTS
- LIVE/VIDEO/REELS - AT LEAST TWICE
- REVIEWED YOUR GOALS
- VISIBLE IN THE 5 GROUPS FOR YOUR IDEAL CUSTOMER
- COMPLETED SOME PERSONAL DEVELOPMENT
- RESPONDED TO COMMENTS AND MESSAGES
- CONNECTED/NETWORKED WITH NEW PEOPLE
- RESPONDED TO COMMENTS AND MESSAGES
- FOLLOWED UP LEADS
- CHECK IN WITH PREVIOUS CUSTOMERS

Weekly Insights

Did you have that lightbulb moment?

My Notes

Weekly Content Planner

Week Commencing
_____

	Monday	Tuesday	Wednesday
Facebook	Posted ☐	Posted ☐	Posted ☐
Twitter	Posted ☐	Posted ☐	Posted ☐
Instagram	Posted ☐	Posted ☐	Posted ☐
LinkedIn	Posted ☐	Posted ☐	Posted ☐
Pinterest	Posted ☐	Posted ☐	Posted ☐
TikTok	Posted ☐	Posted ☐	Posted ☐
Snapchat	Posted ☐	Posted ☐	Posted ☐
Email	Posted ☐	Posted ☐	Posted ☐

Weekly Content Planner

Thursday	Friday	Saturday	Sunday
Posted	Posted	Posted	Posted
Posted	Posted	Posted	Posted
Posted	Posted	Posted	Posted
Posted	Posted	Posted	Posted
Posted	Posted	Posted	Posted
Posted	Posted	Posted	Posted
Posted	Posted	Posted	Posted
Posted	Posted	Posted	Posted

Month: _____

This Week's Priorities
1.
2.
3.
4.
5.

Work To Do List
1.
2.
3.
4.
5.

Personal To Do List
1.
2.
3.
4.
5.

5 Wins
1.
2.
3.
4.
5.

	Monday		Tuesday		Wednesday
Today's Affirmation / Quote		Today's Affirmation / Quote		Today's Affirmation / Quote	
Today's Goal		Today's Goal		Today's Goal	

Monday	Tuesday	Wednesday
06:00	06:00	06:00
06:30	06:30	06:30
07:00	07:00	07:00
07:30	07:30	07:30
08:00	08:00	08:00
08:30	08:30	08:30
09:00	09:00	09:00
09:30	09:30	09:30
10:00	10:00	10:00
10:30	10:30	10:30
11:00	11:00	11:00
11:30	11:30	11:30
12:00	12:00	12:00
12:30	12:30	12:30
13:00	13:00	13:00
13:30	13:30	13:30
14:00	14:00	14:00
14:30	14:30	14:30
15:00	15:00	15:00
15:30	15:30	15:30
16:00	16:00	16:00
16:30	16:30	16:30
17:00	17:00	17:00
17:30	17:30	17:30
18:00	18:00	18:00
18:30	18:30	18:30
19:00	19:00	19:00
19:30	19:30	19:30
20:00	20:00	20:00
20:30	20:30	20:30
21:00	21:00	21:00

NOTES

Post Ideas	Video/Vlogging Ideas	Where I'm Networking	Blogging Ideas

Pink Fizz Social

THURSDAY	FRIDAY	SATURDAY	SUNDAY
Today's Affirmation / Quote	Today's Affirmation / Quote	Today's Affirmation / Quote	Today's Affirmation / Quote
Today's Goal	Today's Goal	Today's Goal	Today's Goal

Thursday	Friday	Saturday	Sunday
06:00	06:00	06:00	06:00
06:30	06:30	06:30	06:30
07:00	07:00	07:00	07:00
07:30	07:30	07:30	07:30
08:00	08:00	08:00	08:00
08:30	08:30	08:30	08:30
09:00	09:00	09:00	09:00
09:30	09:30	09:30	09:30
10:00	10:00	10:00	10:00
10:30	10:30	10:30	10:30
11:00	11:00	11:00	11:00
11:30	11:30	11:30	11:30
12:00	12:00	12:00	12:00
12:30	12:30	12:30	12:30
13:00	13:00	13:00	13:00
13:30	13:30	13:30	13:30
14:00	14:00	14:00	14:00
14:30	14:30	14:30	14:30
15:00	15:00	15:00	15:00
15:30	15:30	15:30	15:30
16:00	16:00	16:00	16:00
16:30	16:30	16:30	16:30
17:00	17:00	17:00	17:00
17:30	17:30	17:30	17:30
18:00	18:00	18:00	18:00
18:30	18:30	18:30	18:30
19:00	19:00	19:00	19:00
19:30	19:30	19:30	19:30
20:00	20:00	20:00	20:00
20:30	20:30	20:30	20:30
21:00	21:00	21:00	21:00

NOTES

Daily Sales	Follow Ups	Product Launches	Other Marketing
Monday			
Tuesday			
Wednesday			
Thursday			
Friday			
Saturday			
Sunday			

Pink Fizz SOCIAL

Weekly Review

Top Ideas of the Week

Useful Links and Resources

Ideas For Future Posts

Total New Followers

Checklist

- Reviewed your insights
- Live/Video/Reels - at least twice
- Reviewed your goals
- Visible in the 5 groups for your ideal customer
- Completed some personal development
- Responded to comments and messages
- Connected/Networked with new people
- Responded to comments and messages
- Followed up leads
- Check in with previous customers

Weekly Insights

Did you have that lightbulb moment?

My Notes

Weekly Content Planner

Week Commencing
_____

	Monday	Tuesday	Wednesday
Facebook	Posted ☐	Posted ☐	Posted ☐
Twitter	Posted ☐	Posted ☐	Posted ☐
Instagram	Posted ☐	Posted ☐	Posted ☐
LinkedIn	Posted ☐	Posted ☐	Posted ☐
Pinterest	Posted ☐	Posted ☐	Posted ☐
TikTok	Posted ☐	Posted ☐	Posted ☐
Snapchat	Posted ☐	Posted ☐	Posted ☐
Email	Posted ☐	Posted ☐	Posted ☐

Weekly Content Planner

Thursday	Friday	Saturday	Sunday
Posted	Posted	Posted	Posted
Posted	Posted	Posted	Posted
Posted	Posted	Posted	Posted
Posted	Posted	Posted	Posted
Posted	Posted	Posted	Posted
Posted	Posted	Posted	Posted
Posted	Posted	Posted	Posted
Posted	Posted	Posted	Posted

MONTH: _____

This Week's Priorities
1.
2.
3.
4.
5.

Work To Do List
1.
2.
3.
4.
5.

Personal To Do List
1.
2.
3.
4.
5.

5 Wins
1.
2.
3.
4.
5.

MONDAY

Today's Affirmation / Quote:

Today's Goal:

Time	
06:00	
06:30	
07:00	
07:30	
08:00	
08:30	
09:00	
09:30	
10:00	
10:30	
11:00	
11:30	
12:00	
12:30	
13:00	
13:30	
14:00	
14:30	
15:00	
15:30	
16:00	
16:30	
17:00	
17:30	
18:00	
18:30	
19:00	
19:30	
20:00	
20:30	
21:00	

TUESDAY

Today's Affirmation / Quote:

Today's Goal:

Time	
06:00	
06:30	
07:00	
07:30	
08:00	
08:30	
09:00	
09:30	
10:00	
10:30	
11:00	
11:30	
12:00	
12:30	
13:00	
13:30	
14:00	
14:30	
15:00	
15:30	
16:00	
16:30	
17:00	
17:30	
18:00	
18:30	
19:00	
19:30	
20:00	
20:30	
21:00	

WEDNESDAY

Today's Affirmation / Quote:

Today's Goal:

Time	
06:00	
06:30	
07:00	
07:30	
08:00	
08:30	
09:00	
09:30	
10:00	
10:30	
11:00	
11:30	
12:00	
12:30	
13:00	
13:30	
14:00	
14:30	
15:00	
15:30	
16:00	
16:30	
17:00	
17:30	
18:00	
18:30	
19:00	
19:30	
20:00	
20:30	
21:00	

NOTES

Post Ideas	Video/Vlogging Ideas	Where I'm Networking	Blogging Ideas

Pink Fizz Social

THURSDAY	FRIDAY	SATURDAY	SUNDAY
Today's Affirmation / Quote	**Today's Affirmation / Quote**	**Today's Affirmation / Quote**	**Today's Affirmation / Quote**
Today's Goal	**Today's Goal**	**Today's Goal**	**Today's Goal**
06:00	06:00	06:00	06:00
06:30	06:30	06:30	06:30
07:00	07:00	07:00	07:00
07:30	07:30	07:30	07:30
08:00	08:00	08:00	08:00
08:30	08:30	08:30	08:30
09:00	09:00	09:00	09:00
09:30	09:30	09:30	09:30
10:00	10:00	10:00	10:00
10:30	10:30	10:30	10:30
11:00	11:00	11:00	11:00
11:30	11:30	11:30	11:30
12:00	12:00	12:00	12:00
12:30	12:30	12:30	12:30
13:00	13:00	13:00	13:00
13:30	13:30	13:30	13:30
14:00	14:00	14:00	14:00
14:30	14:30	14:30	14:30
15:00	15:00	15:00	15:00
15:30	15:30	15:30	15:30
16:00	16:00	16:00	16:00
16:30	16:30	16:30	16:30
17:00	17:00	17:00	17:00
17:30	17:30	17:30	17:30
18:00	18:00	18:00	18:00
18:30	18:30	18:30	18:30
19:00	19:00	19:00	19:00
19:30	19:30	19:30	19:30
20:00	20:00	20:00	20:00
20:30	20:30	20:30	20:30
21:00	21:00	21:00	21:00

NOTES

Daily Sales	Follow Ups	Product Launches	Other Marketing
Monday			
Tuesday			
Wednesday			
Thursday			
Friday			
Saturday			
Sunday			

Pink Fizz SOCIAL

Weekly Review

Top Ideas of the Week

Useful Links and Resources

Ideas For Future Posts

Total New Followers

Checklist

- Reviewed your insights
- Live/Video/Reels - at least twice
- Reviewed your goals
- Visible in the 5 groups for your ideal customer
- Completed some personal development
- Responded to comments and messages
- Connected/Networked with new people
- Responded to comments and messages
- Followed up leads
- Check in with previous customers

Weekly Insights

Did you have that lightbulb moment?

My Notes

Weekly Content Planner

Week Commencing

_____

	Monday	Tuesday	Wednesday
Facebook	Posted ☐	Posted ☐	Posted ☐
Twitter	Posted ☐	Posted ☐	Posted ☐
Instagram	Posted ☐	Posted ☐	Posted ☐
LinkedIn	Posted ☐	Posted ☐	Posted ☐
Pinterest	Posted ☐	Posted ☐	Posted ☐
TikTok	Posted ☐	Posted ☐	Posted ☐
Snapchat	Posted ☐	Posted ☐	Posted ☐
Email	Posted ☐	Posted ☐	Posted ☐

Weekly Content Planner

Thursday	Friday	Saturday	Sunday
Posted ☐	Posted ☐	Posted ☐	Posted ☐
Posted ☐	Posted ☐	Posted ☐	Posted ☐
Posted ☐	Posted ☐	Posted ☐	Posted ☐
Posted ☐	Posted ☐	Posted ☐	Posted ☐
Posted ☐	Posted ☐	Posted ☐	Posted ☐
Posted ☐	Posted ☐	Posted ☐	Posted ☐
Posted ☐	Posted ☐	Posted ☐	Posted ☐
Posted ☐	Posted ☐	Posted ☐	Posted ☐

Month: _____

This Week's Priorities
1.
2.
3.
4.
5.

Work To Do List
1.
2.
3.
4.
5.

Personal To Do List
1.
2.
3.
4.
5.

5 Wins
1.
2.
3.
4.
5.

	MONDAY		TUESDAY		WEDNESDAY
Today's Affirmation / Quote		Today's Affirmation / Quote		Today's Affirmation / Quote	
Today's Goal		Today's Goal		Today's Goal	

Monday	Tuesday	Wednesday
06:00	06:00	06:00
06:30	06:30	06:30
07:00	07:00	07:00
07:30	07:30	07:30
08:00	08:00	08:00
08:30	08:30	08:30
09:00	09:00	09:00
09:30	09:30	09:30
10:00	10:00	10:00
10:30	10:30	10:30
11:00	11:00	11:00
11:30	11:30	11:30
12:00	12:00	12:00
12:30	12:30	12:30
13:00	13:00	13:00
13:30	13:30	13:30
14:00	14:00	14:00
14:30	14:30	14:30
15:00	15:00	15:00
15:30	15:30	15:30
16:00	16:00	16:00
16:30	16:30	16:30
17:00	17:00	17:00
17:30	17:30	17:30
18:00	18:00	18:00
18:30	18:30	18:30
19:00	19:00	19:00
19:30	19:30	19:30
20:00	20:00	20:00
20:30	20:30	20:30
21:00	21:00	21:00

NOTES

Post Ideas	Video/Vlogging Ideas	Where I'm Networking	Blogging Ideas

Pink Fizz Social

Thursday | Friday | Saturday | Sunday

	Thursday	Friday	Saturday	Sunday
Today's Affirmation / Quote				
Today's Goal				
06:00				
06:30				
07:00				
07:30				
08:00				
08:30				
09:00				
09:30				
10:00				
10:30				
11:00				
11:30				
12:00				
12:30				
13:00				
13:30				
14:00				
14:30				
15:00				
15:30				
16:00				
16:30				
17:00				
17:30				
18:00				
18:30				
19:00				
19:30				
20:00				
20:30				
21:00				

NOTES

Daily Sales | **Follow Ups** | **Product Launches** | **Other Marketing**

- Monday
- Tuesday
- Wednesday
- Thursday
- Friday
- Saturday
- Sunday

Pink Fizz Social

Weekly Review

Top Ideas of the Week

Useful Links and Resources

Ideas For Future Posts

Total New Followers

Checklist

- Reviewed your insights
- Live/Video/Reels - at least twice
- Reviewed your goals
- Visible in the 5 groups for your ideal customer
- Completed some personal development
- Responded to comments and messages
- Connected/Networked with new people
- Responded to comments and messages
- Followed up leads
- Check in with previous customers

Weekly Insights

Did you have that lightbulb moment?

My Notes

4 Weekly Reflection

Did I Achieve My Main Focus? _____ If Not Why? _____
_____

What Earnings Did You Reach? _____ Did You Reach Your Goal? _____

How Do I Feel About My Progress

3 Goals I Can Improve On

Lessons Learnt Insights Gained

3 Skills To Improve On

Which Platform Gave Most Visibility

List 5 Types of Post with the Most Engagement

Content Ideas

Go Live and Talk About Your Story	Create a Poll	Ask Your Audience to Join Your Mailing List (If You Haven't Got One Maybe Start One)	Talk About Your Goals
Share a Funny Photo Of You and the Story Behind It	Ask Your Audience What Their Biggest Struggle Is	Interaction Post - Are You an Android or iPhone Fan?	Question - Who is Someone You Look Up Too?
Share a Piece Of Advice That You Have Once Received	Ask Your Audience a Question - If You Sell Make Up for Example - Ask Which Colour Lipstick do They Prefer	Interview a Customer	Share a Sneak Peak Photo - Maybe Something New Your Launching
Talk About Your Product or Services and How They Can Help	Provide a Success Story, This Could Be You or a Success Of One Of Your Customers	Post Something Seasonal	Interaction Post - Would You Rather Be Invisible or Read Minds?
Interaction Post - Ask Your Audience - What Has Your Week Been Like? Explain By Commenting With 5 Emojis Only	Give Something Away (Could Be a Sample, Free Worksheet, Valuable Content, etc)	Share One Of Your Favourite Recipes or Something New You Have Tried	Create a "Day in a Life" Post
Interaction Post - Take Away - Chinese or Indian?	Talk About Your Struggles	Give a Shout Out to Another Local Business	Share an Attention Grabbing Statistic
Share 5 Things About Yourself	Sunday Funday Post	Create a Video, Featuring Your Products, Customers or Testimonials	Thank Your Customers for Their Support
Share Something That's Happening in Your Life Right Now	Post a Start Of the Week Goal Post and Ask Your Audience What Their Goals Are	Share a Motivational Quote	Share an Experience
Interaction Post - What is a Pet Peeve You Can't Stand?	Post Something You Sell or Can Offer for a "Tenner"	Top Tip Tuesday - Share a Quick Tip	Set a Challenge
Interaction Post - What Are You Most Thankful for Today?	Mid Week Check in - Ask Your Audience How Their Week is Going So Far	Promote Your Website	Share Your Top 5 Podcasts to Listen Too
Someone or Something You're Thankful For	Post a Question to Your Audience	What Item From Your Childhood Would Children These Days Not Understand?	Interaction Post - Describe Your Ideal Day
Post a Video That Will Help Get Over the Midweek Hump	Interaction Post - What Song Best Describes Your Week	Share What's On Your Bucket List and Ask Your Audience to Share Theirs	Post Something Educational
Ask Your Audience What Their Favourite Family Activity Is	Post About Something Positive You Have Experienced	Talk About Your Weekend Plans	Share a Tweet You Like
Post a Picture From Wherever You Are Today and Ask Your Audience to Comment and Share Theirs	Share a Puzzle or Riddle	Share a Glimpse Into Your Family Life	Tell a Joke
Question - "What's Your Favourite Motivational Quote? I Could do With a Little Nudge Today"	Share Something You Want to Achieve Before the Age Of __	Get Another Guest Expert to Come Live and Share Some Of Their Expertise and Top Tips in Their Field	Talk About Someone Who Has Inspired You
Share Your Win Of the Week and Ask You Audience What Theirs is Too	Question - I Am Looking for a Movie Recommendation, What do You Recommend?	Interview a Guest	Share a Video Of a Mini Training

For more content ideas visit
https://pinkfizz.social/product/downloads

Printed in Great Britain
by Amazon